MUSICALS

FACTS, FIGURES & FUN

"Any book without a mistake in it has had too much money spent on it"

Sir William Collins, publisher

MUSICALS

FACTS, FIGURES & FUN

MIKE EVANS

ff&f

Musicals
Facts, Figures & Fun

Published by
Facts, Figures & Fun, an imprint of
AAPPL Artists' and Photographers' Press Ltd.
10 Hillside, London SW19 4NH, UK
info@ffnf.co.uk www.ffnf.co.uk
info@aappl.com www.aappl.com

Sales and Distribution
UK and export: Turnaround Publisher Services Ltd.
orders@turnaround-uk.com
USA and Canada: Sterling Publishing Inc. sales@sterlingpub.com
Australia & New Zealand: Peribo Pty. peribomec@bigpond.com
South Africa: Trinity Books. trinity@iafrica.com

A catalogue record for this book is available from the
British Library.

ISBN 13: 9781904332381
ISBN 10: 1904332382

Design (contents and cover): Malcolm Couch
mal.couch@blueyonder.co.uk

Printed in China by Imago Publishing
info@imago.co.uk

For information about custom editions, special sales, premium
and corporate purchases, please contact ffnf Special Sales
+44 20 8971 2094 or info@ffnf.co.uk

CONTENTS

ORIGINS OF THE MUSICAL

The modern musical has its roots in various strands of popular entertainment which flourished in Europe and subsequently the United States. These ranged from operetta and comic opera which thrived from the 1700s in Britain France and elsewhere, to the Music Hall and Vaudeville on either side of the Atlantic in the late 19th and early 20th century.

COMIC OPERA, LIGHT OPERA AND OPERETTA

From the 18th century, two forms of comic opera were popular. There were "low comedies" in which the lyrics of popular songs were rewritten to fit a particular plot; in England the best known example of this was John Gay's *The Beggar's Opera* (1728). And there were "high comedies" like *The Bohemian Girl* by Michael Balfe (1845), with original music and usually more romantic plot lines.

☆

In France, the genre's greatest name was Jaques Offenbach (1819-1880), whose long string of hit operettas included 1858's *Orpheus in the Underworld* and *La Belle Helene* (1864), which took a comic look at the legend of Helen of Troy.

Known as "The Waltz King", Johann Strauss II was the most successful musician of his time, his waltzes such as 'The Blue Danube' and 'The Emperor Waltz' being the pop music of the day. He also admired Offenbach's operettas, and when he attempted one of his own – with a script by the French composer's librettists – the result was the hugely popular *Die Fledermaus* (*The Bat*) in 1874.

··············· GILBERT & SULLIVAN ···············

When writer William S. Gilbert (1836-1911) collaborated with the composer Arthur S. Sullivan (1842-1900) on *Thespis* in 1871, it was the beginning of a working relationship which produced a total of 14 light operas over the next 25 years. Most of these were written for Richard D'Oyly Carte's company at London's Savoy Theatre, the company having absolute control on how the works were produced until the copyright expired in 1961.

Despite their highly stylised form and mannered songs, Gilbert & Sullivan operettas like *The Mikado* and *The Yeomen of the Guard* (the nearest G&S got to a full-blown opera) were the first true blockbusters in British musical theatre, and continue to be hugely popular with amateur and professional theatre companys worldwide.

After the Gilbert and Sullivan shows were "liberated" from the rigid strictures of D'Oyly Carte, all manner of variations were produced, some more successful than others. These included a London all-black version of *The Mikado* entitled   *The Black Mikado* in 1975, and a Broadway revival of *The Pirates of Penzance*. The latter certainly fared better than its movie spin-off (starring Kevin Kline and rock singer Linda Ronstadt),

---

G&S's GREATEST HITS

TITLE / OPENING DATE / THEATRE
FIRST RUN PERFORMANCES

The Mikado 14 March 1885, Savoy 672

H.M.S. Pinafore 25 May 1878, Opera Comique 571

The Gondoliers 7 December 1889, Savoy 554

The Yeomen of the Guard 3 October 1888, Savoy 423

Pirates of Penzance 2 April 1880, Opera Comique 363

---

about which *The Observer* commented "Anyone who thinks Gilbert and Sullivan indestructable should see this."

Light opera continued to flourish well into the 20th century. Prague-trained composer Franz Lehar (1870-1948) caught the mood of Edwardian England perfectly in *The Merry Widow*, a London stage hit in 1907. And another Prague graduate, Rudolph Friml (1879-1972) kept the flag of traditional light opera flying in New York into the Twenties with his hits *Rose Marie* (1924) and *The Vagabond King* (1925). Also an eastern European émigré to the United States, Sigmund Romberg's first hit on the New York stage was *Maytime* in 1917, followed by even bigger smashes in *The Student Prince* (1924) and 1926's *The Desert Song*.

> *"I am terrified at the thought that so much hideous*
> *and bad music will be put on records forever."*
> Arthur Sullivan

·················· PANTOMIME ··················

Musical pantomimes had been a feature of the London stage since the 18th century. They were initially one-act playlets sharing the bill with other novelty entertainments, in mixed-bag productions which were precursors to the music hall and variety theatre. In the pantomimes, characters from "Mother Goose" fairy stories were presented in various settings, where a fairy queen (later a fairy godmother) would transform them into roles from the traditional *commedia dell' arte* – Harlequin, Columbine, Clown and such. The clowns then indulged in various escapades and misunderstandings, using only mimed gestures and slapstick.

The most successful American pantomime in the 19th century was *Humpty Dumpty*, which ran from 1868 with comic actor George Fox in the title role. The plot turned young Humpty and his friends into harlequinade characters, romping through a variety of settings including a candy store, an enchanted garden and even Manhattan's expensive new City Hall.

In the UK, "panto" as it became familiarly known evolved into a children-oriented parallel of the variety theatre, staged over the Christmas-New Year period. In recent years it has become a vehicle for various (mainly televison) celebrities to ham it up as the principal boy (played by a female), pantomime dame (played by a man), the villains, fairy godmother and so on.

According to a BBC survey, the most popular panto is *Cinderella*, followed by *Aladdin*, *Dick Whittington* and *Snow White*. Other popular titles are *Jack & the Beanstalk*, *Babes in the Wood*, and *Sleeping Beauty*. *Peter Pan* is gaining in popularity, although purists would argue that this is not strictly a pantomime, but a children's story.

OH YES IT WAS.....!!
THE OLDEST PANTO STORIES

Babes in the Wood
First appeared in England 500 years ago.

Puss in Boots
Over 450 years old

Sleeping Beauty
Over 450 years old

Aladdin and His Magic Lamp
1717, Arabian Nights translated into English

Sinbad the Sailor
1717, Arabian Nights translated into English

Ali Baba and the Forty Thieves
1717, Arabian Nights translated into English

Dick Whittington
19th century

Robinson Crusoe
19th century

Robin Hood
19th century

MINSTREL SHOWS

In the United States, where they originated, minstrel shows (or minstrelsy) were the most popular form of musical stage entertainment in the mid-19th century. They began in the 1830s -- a performer called Dan Emmet claimed to have originated the form – with working class white men dressing up as plantation slaves, parodying black music and dance in an often savage mockery. By the time of the Civil War these shows had become world famous and thoroughly respectable, the white performers "blacking up" their faces with burnt cork or grease-paint and dressing in outlandish costumes, performing songs that played on racial stereotypes of the still-enslaved Black Americans.

The shows' popularity spread after the Civil War, with stock characters in the skits and routines that included "Mr Tambo", a happy-go-lucky musician (usually playing a banjo), "Mr Bones" who played two bones like castanets, "Zip Coon" a liberated slave trying to rise above his station by "putting on airs", and "Jim Crow", the caricature carefree slave. "Jim Crow" originated in 1828 with a white blackface performer Thomas "Daddy" Rice, who would dance a grotesque jig while singing the song 'Jump Jim Crow'. The character became so well-known, and associated with racial bigotry, that after emancipation the phrase was adopted as a derogatory reference to the segregation laws and customs that bedevilled the South until the 1960s.

TOP TEN FOSTER FAVOURITES

Oh! Susanna 1848

Camptown Races 1850

Old Folks At Home [aka *Swanee River*] 1851

Ring, Ring De Banjo! 1851

My Old Kentucky Home, Good-Night! 1853

Jeanie With The Light Brown Hair 1854

Gentle Annie 1856

Beautiful Dreamer 1862

The Voices That Are Gone 1865

Old Black Joe 1860

Some of the most famous songs in American history, such as 'Dixie', 'Camptown Races', 'Oh Sussanah' and My Old Kentucky Home', began as minstrel tunes. Many of the most popular of these came from the pen of one man, Stephen Foster (1826-64), a Northerner who captured what was naively thought of as a Southern plantation "spirit" that was far removed from the reality.

Before the Civil War, black men were prohibited from performing in minstrel shows even if they had wished to, but later in the 19th century there were many instances of black performers putting on minstrel make-up and appearing as white men imitating black men! And in the 20th century several of the most famous minstrels were black men "blacked-up", including Bert Williams who performed into the Twenties.

In America minstrel shows continued to be popular as song-and-dance entertainments into the Fifties, after which they were seen to be at odds with the spirit of the Civil Rights era. Controversially, in Britain the BBC continued running its *Black And White Minstrel Show* on television until the late Seventies.

MUSIC HALL & VAUDEVILLE

While access to grand opera was strictly for the well-to-do, and operetta the toast of the middle classes, the Music Hall was where the British working class got their main taste of musical theatre in the Victorian and Edwardian era.

With such stars as Marie Lloyd, George Robey and the archetypal Scotsman Harry Lauder, the Music Hall circuit extended into every city and town, and offered a straightforward formula of basic – often bawdy – humour and sentimental song. It was a key factor in the launching of "Tin Pan Alley" popular music, and was a direct forerunner of the variety theatre which took its place after World War I.

TEN TOP TUNES
FROM THE MUSIC HALL
Featured by

After The Ball
Vesta Tilley (1864-1952)

Any Old Iron
Harry Champion (1866-1942)

Boiled Beef And Carrots
Harry Champion

If You Were The Only Girl In The World
George Robey (1869-1954)

Glasgow Belongs To Me
Harry Lauder (1870-1950)

Roamin' In The Gloamin'
Harry Lauder

Knocked 'Em In The Old Kent Road
Albert Chevalier (1861-1923)

Oh! Mr Porter
Marie Lloyd (1870-1922)

The Man Who Broke The Bank At Monte Carlo
Charles Coburn (1852-1945)

The Old Bull And Bush
Florrie Ford (1876-1940)

As well as UK recording and film stars like Flanangan & Allen, George Formby and Gracie Fields, the British Music Hall produced future Hollywood movie legends in Stan Laurel and Charlie Chaplin.

The American parallel to the British Music Hall was Vaudeville, which evolved from the travelling medicine shows that toured the Mid West through the 19th century. It featured a similar mix to Music Hall, of slapstick comedy, acrobatic and juggling acts, but with the main emphasis on song and dance.

George M Cohan (1878-1942) was a song & dance man and producer who developed his Vaudeville sketches into highly successful Broadway musicals, the first being *Little Johnny Jones* in 1904. Songs from the show included 'Meet Me In St Louis', 'Yankee Doodle Dandy' and 'Give My Regards To Broadway', all of which became evergreeens. The importance of Cohan lay in his injecting the Broadway stage with the vitality of Vaudeville, thereby creating an audience for the "book" musical in a theatrical environment attuned to the more staid conventions of operetta. His life in show biz was celebrated in the 1942 film *Yankee Doodle Dandy*, with James Cagney in an Oscar-winning role as Cohan.

Vaudeville's other contribution to the Broadway musical as we know it was via the Follies. Pioneered by Florenz Ziegfeld, the annual *Ziegfeld Follies* (the first of which was in 1907) ran until his death in 1932. The spectacular revues which featured over 50 showgirls, were a springboard for Broadway legends like "Funny Girl" Fanny Brice, and composers such as Irving Berlin who went on to be architects of the musicals that followed.

THE CLASSIC MUSICAL

In the wake of the continuing success of light operas like Rudolph Friml's *Rose Marie*, a Broadway hit in 1924, the musical as we know it burst onto the New York and London stage in the Twenties and has reigned supreme as the most enduring form of musical theatre ever since.

One of the first big hits on both sides of the Atlantic was *No, No, Nanette* in 1925. Written by Irving Caesar and Otto Harbach with music by Vincent Youmans, the trite tale of a businessman with a penchant for pretty girls scored by virtue of its songs, which included 'I Want To Be Happy' and 'Tea For Two'. Much to the chagrin of the Broadway producers, the original US production was so successful touring that it hit London before New York. It was later loosely adapted as the 1950 film *Tea For Two* with Doris Day and Gordon MacRae.

·············· ON BROADWAY ··············

WHY BROADWAY?
Broadway actually stretches the entire 11-mile length of Manhattan Island, top to bottom, and has its start way north of that on the mainland of New York State.

MUSICALS: A BRIEF GLOSSARY

Book	The story and spoken dialogue in a musical
Choreographer	The person who arranges the dance sequences
Conductor	He or she conducts the pit orchestra and any on-stage choral singers
Dance Captain	Someone who rehearses the dancers in the absence of the choreographer
Director	The person in command of what happens on stage, and has a big say in the casting of the parts
Eleven o'clock number	A final show-stopper (see below) that climaxes the performance
Libretto	The same as "lyrics", but applied to opera or operetta
Lyrics	The words of the songs
Matinée	A performance in the daytime

Pit	Where the band or orchestra usually performs from in front of, and below the level of, the stage
Preview	A performance before the official opening of a show
Producer	The person who buys the property (see below), raises the money, books the theatre, contracts the director and performers, and arranges the publicity
Property	The whole package of music, lyrics and book
Revue	A show featuring a series of unrelated sketches, songs and dances
Score	The entire musical content and their arrangements for instruments and voices
Show-stopper	A song that literally stops a show by receiving lengthy applause
Understudy	A performer who learns another's role in order to take over at short notice when necessary

The theatre in New York has been associated with Broadway since the 19th century, but it wasn't always the prime centre. Previously Manhattan's musical theatreland was concentrated on the Bowery on the Lower East Side, and later the Chelsea area around West 23rd Street.

The Bowery, which later became a notoriously run-down area but is now enjoying a revival, was the hub of New York's Vaudeville – and its seedier cousin, the burlesque revue – from the late 19th century. Then the focus turned to West 23rd Street, where prestigious venues like Koster and Bial's variety theatre flourished, before the "district" moved yet again up to midtown locations around 40th Street in the early 20th century.

It was there that Broadway – or at least that stretch of Broadway that runs from 40th Street up through Times Square to the middle 50s – got its nickname The Great White Way, on account of the neon-lit illuminations of the theatres, as it became the glittering nerve centre of the stage musical.

Nearly two hundred theatres have fourished on and near Broadway over the past century. At least 44 of them are currently functioning as theatres, while another eight or so are former theatrical venues that are still standing. In addition, about 140 establishments have been demolished over the years.

Broadway Divas

Julie Andrews
Born: Julia Wells, 1 October, 1935, Walton-on-Thames, Surrey
Major Broadway Shows: The Boy Friend (1954), My Fair Lady (1956), Camelot (1960)

THE LONGEST RUNS ON BROADWAY

The totals for number of performances do not include previews. Broadway shows generally play eight performances a week, or about 416 performances per year.

These figures are as of July 31, 2005. Shows marked with an asterisk (★) are still running.

MUSICAL	RUN	YEAR	THEATRE
Cats	7,485	1982	Winter Garden
★The Phantom of the Opera	7,301	1988	Majestic
Les Miserables	6,680	1987	Broadway
A Chorus Line	6,137	1975	Shubert
Oh! Calcutta! *(revival)*	5,959	1971	Belasco,
		1976	Edison
★ Beauty and the Beast	4,632	1994	Palace
Miss Saigon	4,097	1991	Broadway
★Rent	3,865	1996	Nederlander
★Chicago *(revival)*	3,618	1996	Shubert
42nd Street	3,486	1980	Winter Garden
Grease *(original production)*	3,388	1972	Eden
★The Lion King	3,250	1997	New Amsterdam
Fiddler on the Roof	3,242	1964	Imperial
Hello, Dolly!	2,844	1964	St. James
My Fair Lady	2,717	1956	Mark Hellinger
Cabaret *(revival)*	2,378	1998	Henry Miller, Studio 54
Annie	2,377	1977	Alvin
Man of La Mancha	2,328	1965	ANTA, Washington Sq.
Oklahoma!	2,212	1943	St. James
Smokey Joe's Cafe	2,036	1995	Virginia

Gertrude Lawrence
Born: Gertrude Alexandra Dagmar Lawrence Klasen, 4 July 1898, London
Died: 6 September 1952, New York City
Major Broadway Shows: Oh, Kay! (1926), Lady In The Dark (1941), The King and I (1951)

Mary Martin
Born: Mary Virginia Martin, 1 December 1913, Weatherford, Texas
Died: 3 November 1990, Rancho Mirage, California
Major Broadway Shows: Leave It To Me (1938), One Touch Of Venus (1943), South Pacific (1949), Peter Pan (1954), The Sound Of Music (1959)

Ethel Merman
Born: Ethel Agnes Zimmerman, 18 January 1908, New York City
Died: 15 February 1984, New York City
Major Broadway Shows: Anything Goes (1934), Annie Get Your Gun (1946), Call Me Madam (1950), Gypsy (1959)

Gwen Verdon
Born: Gwyneth Evelyn Verdon, 13 January 1926, Culver City, California
Died: 18 October 2000, Woodstock, Vermont
Major Broadway Shows: Can-Can (1953), Damn Yankees (1955), Sweet Charity (1966), Chicago (1975)

TOP OF THE FLOPS

There have been many theatrical disasters in the history of the musical. Famous flops in London have included *Which Witch* (1992), a story about a medieval witch by Norwegians Ingrid Bjornov and Benedicte Adrian (famous for scoring "nul points" in the 1984 Eurovision Song Contest), and *The Fields of Ambrosia* (1996), about a travelling executioner !

One of the biggest flops on Broadway was *1600 Pennsylvania Avenue* in 1976. With lyrics by Alan J. Lerner (of *My Fair Lady* and *Brigadoon* fame) and music by Leonard Bernstein (we're talking *On the Town* and *West Side Story* in his case), it should have been a runaway success. But the only thing running away was the producer's money, when it closed after just seven performances.

One of the biggest box office bombshells ever to hit Broadway was with *Carrie* – produced by Britain's Royal Shakespeare Company in 1988 – a musical adaptation of Stephen King's horror novel of the same name. Starring Betty Buckley, the show closed after only five performances. Writing in the *New York Daily News*, critic Howard Kissel confessed "For me the high point of the lyrics was rhyming 'attitude' with 'I've been screwed'"

Even *Carrie* couldn't compete with *La Strada* however, for the all-time shortest run. Written by Lionel Bart and based on the Federico Fellini film, it ran just one night on 14 December 1969. And a similar fate befell *Oscar*, penned by Mike Read and based on the life of Oscar Wilde. The show – which opened at London's Shaw Theatre in October 2004 – closed after its opening night, having received universally bad notices from the critics.

LEGENDARY MUSICALS:
SHOW BOAT

Considered the first of the truly classic musicals, *Show Boat* heralded the golden era of Broadway shows with memorable songs and an equally strong storyline. Set on a Mississippi theatre show boat, the role of stevedore Joe (who famously ends the performance with 'Ol' Man River') was originally earmarked for singer Paul Robeson; he didn't make the Broadway production, but starred in the West End run and later the 1936 film.

Lyrics: Oscar Hammerstein II
Music: Jerome Kern
Book: Oscar Hammerstein II, based on Edna Furber novel *Show Boat*

First Performance:
New York, 20 December 1927, Ziegfeld Theater (572 performances)
London, 3 May 1928, Drury Lane Theatre, (350 performances)

Hit songs: 'Make Believe', 'Can't Help Lovin' Dat Man', 'Why Do I Love You', 'Bill', 'Ol' Man River'.

Film version: 1929 (Laura La Plante, Joseph Schildkraut. Director Harry Pollard), 1936 (Irene Dunne, Allan Jones. Director James Whale) and 1951 (Kathryn Grayson, Howard Keel. Director George Sidney)

The 1929 movie version of *Show Boat* was actually a silent film, with a sound prologue sung by members of the cast.

Before he became a huge movie star, dancer Fred Astaire was a big name in Vaudeville and then Broadway shows, teamed with his sister Adele. The partnership ended when she retired to marry an English aristocrat, their last New York appearance being in 1931's *The Band Wagon*. It was basically a revue, but later became a "book" musical when transferred to the screen in 1953 – and about which critic Archer Winsten raved "The best musical of the month, the year, the decade, or for all I know of all time".

Although he'd made a minor impression on the Great White Way with *See America First* in 1916, songwriter Cole Porter broke through on Broadway with no less than four hit shows and over 750 performances in the period 1928-1930. Living a playboy-style life in Paris, Venice and the French Riviera, after the shows *Paris*, *The New Yorkers*, *Fifty Million Frenchmen* and *Wake Up and Dream* made his name he immediately settled in Manhattan's smart Waldorf-Astoria hotel and established himself as possibly the greatest composer of popular song – before or since.

PROFILE: **COLE PORTER**

Born: 9 June 1991, Peru, Indiana
Died: 15 October 1964, Santa Monica, California

Major Shows: The Gay Divorce (1932), Anything Goes (1934), Kiss Me Kate (1948), Can Can (1953), Silk Stockings (1955)

Major Films: The Pirate (1948), Kiss Me Kate (1953), High Society (1956), Les Girls (1957), Can Can (1960)

Memorable Songs: I'm In Love Again (1924), Let's Do It (1928), You Do Something To Me, What Is This Thing Called Love? (1929), Love For Sale (1930), Night And Day (1932), Anything Goes, I Get A Kick Out Of You, You're The Top (1934), Begin The Beguine, Just One Of Those Things (1935), Every Time We Say Goodbye (1944), From This Moment On (1950), I Love Paris, C'est Magnifique, (1953), Well Did You Evah!, Who Wants To Be A Millionaire, True Love (1956)

The Thirties were also a peak period for the songwriting team of Rodgers and Hart. In 1935 an extravaganza set in the circus (with a real life elephant, Paul Whiteman's famous orchestra *and* star comic Jimmy Durante) called *Jumbo* was the unlikely setting for standards-to-be 'The Most Beautiful Girl In The World' and 'My Romance'. The following year *On Your Toes* brought a ballet storyline to Broadway, featuring 'There's A Small Hotel' and the evocative climax of 'Slaughter On Tenth Avenue'.

PROFILE: **RODGERS & HART**

Richard Rodgers
Born: 28 June 1902, Long Island, New York
Died: 30 December 1979, New York City

Lorentz Hart
Born: 2 May 1895, New York City
Died: 22 November 1943, New York City

Major Shows: Jumbo (1935), On Your Toes (1936), Babes In Arms (1937), The Boys From Syracuse (1938), Pal Joey (1940)

Major Films: The Boys From Syracuse (1940), Pal Joey (1957)

Memorable Songs: The Most Beautiful Girl In The World, My Romance (1935), There's A Small Hotel (1936), I Wish I Were In Love Again, My Funny Valentine, Where Or When, The Lady Is A Tramp (1937), Falling In Love With Love (1938), I Could Write A Book, Chicago, Bewitched Bothered And Bewildered (1940)

"In America the musical theater is generally considered a whore.
My ambition is to help make a good woman of her."
Richard Rodgers

In 1937 Rodgers and Hart surpassed themselves with *Babes In Arms*, a piece of youthful escapism that featured no less than four all-time classic numbers – 'I Wish I Were In Love Again', 'My Funny Valentine', 'Where Or When' and 'The Lady Is A Tramp'. A perfect example of the songs far outliving the shows, which was often the case before World War II. It was in the Forties, Fifties and thereafter that many of the musicals became as immortal as the songs.

LEGENDARY MUSICALS:
PAL JOEY

Way ahead of it's time, Rogers and Hart's masterpiece *Pal Joey* didn't do that well at the box office when it opened in 1940. Critics were muted in their praise of a musical which went against the grain with a basically "unlikeable" lead character in Joey Evans, a wheeling and dealing dancer who used the women around him to his own ends. Despite a great portrayal by Gene Kelly, it took a 1952 revival to establish it as a ground-breaking classic. The Frank Sinatra film in 1957 watered-down some of the plot in deference to the censors, but beefed up the score with additional Rogers and Hart standards.

Lyrics: Lorentz Hart
Music: Richard Rodgers
Book: John O'Hara, based on his short stories

First Performance:
New York, 25 December 1940, Ethel Barrymore (374 performances)
London, 31 March 1954, Princes Theatre, (245 performances)

Hit songs: *'.I Could Write A Book', 'Chicago', 'Bewitched Bothered And Bewildered'.*

Film version: 1957 (Frank Sinatra, Rita Hayworth. Director George Sidney

The Rodgers and Hart partnership broke up in 1942 when the latter decided he wasn't interested in an adaptation of a flop play *Green Grow The Lilacs*. Consequently Rodgers found it hard to get backers for the project, especially as he'd teamed up with Oscar Hammerstein II, who hadn't had a success since *Show Boat* over a decade earlier. But Rodgers perservered, and the result − *Oklahoma!* − turned out to be one of the most successful musicals of all time.

After 2,212 performances on Broadway, 1,548 in London, thousands more touring and a blockbuster screen version, *Oklahoma!* grossed over $100 million dollars − and that was before any later revivals. The show held the record for the longest-running Broadway musical for fifteen years before being beaten by *My Fair Lady*.

In 1953, the title song from *Oklahoma!* became the official song of the state of Oklahoma.

LEGENDARY MUSICALS:
OKLAHOMA!

The prarie-based romantic story set to music marked a radical breakthrough in the stage musical, with its dynamic integration of book, song and dance on a scale not seen previously. As with many shows that followed, its narrative strength enabled it to transfer to the Hollywood screen virtually unchanged.

Lyrics: Oscar Hammerstein II
Music: Richard Rodgers
Book: Oscar Hammerstein II, based on *Green Grow The Lilacs* by Lynn Riggs.

First Performance:
New York, 31 March 1943, St James Theater (2212 performances)
London, 29 April 1947, Drury Lane Theatre, (1548 perform-
ances)

Hit songs: *'. Oh What A Beautiful Morning', 'People Will Say We're In Love', 'The Surrey With The Fringe On Top', 'Oklahoma!'.*

Film version: 1955 (Gordon Macrae, Shirley Jones. Director Fred Zinnemann)

In its initial try-outs, Oklahoma was actually known as *Away We Go*

Following *Oklahoma!*, Rodgers and Hammerstein could seem-ngly do no wrong, with *Carousel* (1945), *South Pacific* (1949) and *The King And I* (1951) all huge successes,   the four shows totalling nearly 6300 performances in their original Broadway productions and over 10,000 including their first runs in London's West End.

Although it was the great era of the rock'n'roll revolution, the album charts in the Fifties were dominated by film and stage musicals. Of the top ten best sellers of the decade, no less than seven – *South Pacific, Love Me Or Leave Me, My Fair Lady, The Music Man, Around The World In 80 Days, Gigi* and *Peter Gunn* – were original stage casts or soundtrack recordings.

Carousel gave the world of soccer it's most famous anthem, after Liverpool FC fans adopted 'You'll Never Walk Alone' in the Sixties, from the hit recording by local group Gerry & the Pacemakers.

South Pacific set the record for the greatest advance ticket sales for any Broadway show up to that point.

The King And I was actually initiated by Gertrude Lawrence (who played the female lead Anna), who originally wanted Cole Porter to write the music. She needn't have worried: the show's final score, which included 'Getting To Know You', 'Shall We Dance', and 'Hello Young Lovers', simply couldn't have been bettered.

The part of the King of Siam in *The King And I,* made famous on the stage and screen by Yul Brynner, was turned down by a number of actors, including Noël Coward.

PROFILE: RODGERS & HAMMERSTEIN

Richard Rodgers
Born: 28 June 1902, Long Island, New York
Died: 30 December 1979, New York City

Oscar Hammerstein II
Born: 12 July 1895, New York City
Died: 23 August 1960, Doylestown, Pennsylvania

Major Shows: Oklahoma! (1943), Carousel (1945), South Pacific (1949), The King And I (1951), Flower Drum Song (1958), The Sound Of Music (1959).

Major Films: Oklahoma! (1955), Carousel, The King And I (1956), South Pacific (1958), The Sound Of Music (1965)

Memorable Songs: Oh What A Beautiful Morning, People Will Say We're In Love, The Surrey With The

Fringe On Top, Oklahoma! (1943), If I Loved You, You'll
Never Walk Alone (1945), Some Enchanted Evening,
There's Nothing Like A Dame, Younger Than Springtime,
I'm Gonna Wash That Man Right Out Of My Hair
(1949), Getting To Know You, Shall We Dance, Hello
Young Lovers (1951), I Enjoy Being A Girl (1958), My
Favourite Things, The Sound Of Music, Do-Re-Mi,
Climb Every Mountain (1959)

> *"The number of people who will not go to a show*
> *they do not want to see is unlimited. "*
> Oscar Hammerstein II

The film soundtrack of *South Pacific* still holds the UK record
for the most weeks in the Number One spot in the album
charts. At 115 weeks it's way ahead of the runners-up – Simon
& Garfunkel's *Bridge Over Troubled Water* (41 weeks) and The
Beatles' *Please Please Me* (30 weeks). It also holds the record for
most consecutive weeks in the top spot (70), with the Beatles'
Please Please Me trailing second with 30 straight weeks at the
top.

LEGENDARY MUSICALS:

SOUTH PACIFIC

A musical drama set on a Pacific island during World War II,
where a romance among the American forces stationed there is
hindered by small-town prejudice on the part of nurse Nellie
Forbush who falls in love with an older man, a local planter. No
such problem occurs to Lieutenant Joe Cable who's in love
with a Polynesian girl, but who tragically is killed on a spy
mission to a neighboring island.

Lyrics: Oscar Hammerstein II
Music: Richard Rodgers

Book: Oscar Hammerstein II and Joshua Logan, based on stories from James Michener's *Tales of the South Pacific*.

First Performance:
New York, 7 April 1949, Majestic Theater (1925 performances)
London, 1 Novmber 1951, Drury Lane Theatre, (802 performances)

Hit songs: *'Some Enchanted Evening', 'There's Nothing Like A Dame', Younger Than Springtime', 'Bali Hai', 'I'm Gonna Wash That Man Right Out Of My Hair'*

Film version: 1958 (Mitzi Gaynor, Rossano Brazzi. Director, Joshua Logan)

During the original London run of South Pacific, at one point Sean Connery was a member of the chorus

The Forties saw a stage comeback of a composer who's name had first been in lights in 1910 with a revue called *Up And Down Broadway*, Irving Berlin. He'd had his first complete Broadway show in 1914, hot on the heels of his hit song 'Alexander's Ragtime Band' (1911). Then after contributing to the *Ziegfeld Follies* regularly, he concentrated on Hollywood musicals in the Thirties, most noteably *Top Hat* (1935) and *Follow The Fleet* (1936). Then, in 1946, he took over a project earmarked for Jerome Kern that would be his most successful Broadway show – *Annie Get Your Gun*.

PROFILE: **IRVING BERLIN**

Born: Israel Baline, 11 May 1888, Temun, Siberia, Russia
Died: 22 September 1989, New York City

Major Shows: This Is The Army (1942), Annie Get Your Gun (1946), Call Me Madam (1950)

Major Films: Top Hat (1935), Holiday Inn (1942), Easter Parade (1948), Annie Get Your Gun (1950), There's No Business Like Show Business (1954), White Christmas (1954)

Memorable Songs: Alexander's Ragtime Band (1911), White Christmas (1942), They Say It's Wonderful, There's No Business Like Show Business, I Got the Sun In The Morning (1946)

LEGENDARY MUSICALS:
ANNIE GET YOUR GUN

Set in Buffalo Bill's travelling Wild West Show, the fairly conventional storyline concerns the rivalry – and inevitable love affair – between sharp-shooters Annie Oakley and Frank Butler. This was truly a case where the success of a musical lay not so much in the plot but the wonderful score.

Lyrics: Irving Berlin
Music: Irving Berlin
Book: Herbert and Dorothy Fields

First Performance:
New York, 16 May 1946, Imperial Theater (1147 performances)
London, 7 June 1947, Coliseum, (1304 performances)

Hit songs: 'The Girls That I Marry', 'My Defences Are Down', 'Anything You Can Do', 'They Say It's Wonderful', 'I Got The Sun In The Morning', 'There's No Business like Show Business'

Film version: 1950 (Betty Hutton, Howard Keel. Director, George Sydney)

Judy Garland was originally earmarked for the lead part in the movie of *Annie Get Your Gun,* but her personal problems ruled her out and the role went to Betty Hutton, who gave the best performance of her film career.

Annie Get Your Gun used a tried and tested formula of a "show-within-a-show", in this case Buffalo Bill's Wild West Show. Other famous musicals that adopted the same device included 1937's *Babes In Arms* by Rodgers and Hart, in which the kids stage the archetypal "show in the barn", and Cole Porter's *Kiss Me Kate* (1948), where the characters are putting on a musical version of Shakespeare's *Taming Of The Shrew*.

BRUSH UP YOUR SHAKESPEARE

Kiss Me Kate (in which 'Brush Up Your Shakespeare' was a hit song) was just one of several musicals based on works by the Bard of Avon.

DATE / MUSICAL / COMPOSER / BASED ON

1938 **The Boys from Syracuse** Rodgers & Hart
Comedy of Errors

1948 **Kiss Me Kate** Cole Porter
Taming of the Shrew

1957 **West Side Story** Sondheim-Bernstein
Romeo and Juliet

1971 **Two Gentlemen of Verona** Galt McDermott
Two Gentlemen of Verona

1971 **The Tale of Cymbeline** Galt McDermott
Cymbeline

1976 **Rockabye Hamlet** Cliff Jones
Hamlet

1968 **Your Own Thing** Hester-Apolonar
Twelfth Night

2000 **Play On!** Sheldon Epps
Twelfth Night

2002 **Illyria** Peter Mills
Twelfth Night

One of the biggest successes of the classic era was another adaptation, this time of *Pygmalion* by George Bernard Shaw. In *My Fair Lady*, Alan J Lerner and Frederick Loewe took the "story" musical to new heights in the tale of the London flower girl who's taught to "speak proper" by elocutionist Professor Higgins.

A radical step was taken in casting *My Fair Lady* when the role of Professor Higgins was given to a straight actor, Rex Harrison, rather than a singer/actor. So successful was his Broadway performance – and that of Julie Andrews who'd only appeared in New York once before, in *The Boy Friend* – that they both starred in the production when it moved to London two years later.

LEGENDARY MUSICALS:

MY FAIR LADY

Pygmalion, the Shaw play from which it was adapted was left virtually intact, with the songs being skillfully integrated, and the whole production enhanced no small way by Moss Hart's direction, Oliver Smith's marvellous sets and costumes designed by Cecil Beaton.

Lyrics: Allan Jay Lerner
Music: Frederick Loewe
Book: Allan Jay Lerner, after George Bernard Shaw's play *Pygmalion*.

First Performance:
New York, 15 March 1956, Mark Hellinger Theater (2717 performances)
London, 30 April 1958, Drury Lane Theatre (2281 performances)

Hit songs: 'Wouldn't It Be Loverly', 'On The Street Where You

Live', 'With A Little Bit Of Luck', 'I Could Have Danced All Night'

Film version: 1964 (Rex Harrison, Audrey Hepburn. Director, George Cukor)

The Broadway cast recording of *My Fair Lady* spent nearly 300 weeks in the US album chart, 15 of them in the Number 1 position.

> *"I absolutely forbid any such outrage."*
> George Bernard Shaw, on turning his *Pygmalion* into a musical

Shakespeare and Shaw weren't the only writers who were adapted for the musical in the wake of *My Fair Lady*, with at least 25 shows based on literary works. These were the most successful:

DATE / MUSICAL / BASED ON / ORIGINAL AUTHOR
1963 **Half A Sixpence** *Kipps* H.G. Wells
1963 **Oliver!** *Oliver Twist* Charles Dickens
1964 **Hello Dolly** *The Matchmaker* Thornton Wilder
1965 **The Man of La Mancha** *Don Quixote*
Miguel de Cervantes
1966 **Cabaret** *Goodbye to Berlin* Christopher Isherwood
1966 **Mame** *Auntie Mame* Patrick Dennis
1969 **Billy** *Billy Budd* Herman Melville

and later adaptations from classic books have included:
1981 **Cats** *Old Possum's Book of Practical Cats* T.S. Elliott
1986 **Phantom of the Opera** *Phantom of the Opera*
Gaston Leroux
1987 **Les Miserables** *Les Miserables* Victor Hugo
2004 **The Woman In White** *The Woman In White*
Wilkie Collins

The best-known stage musical of J.M.Barrie's *Peter Pan* was the 1954 New York production starring Mary Martin and choreographed by Jerome Robbins, but a previous Broadway version from 1950 had music by Leonard Bernstein and Dr Hook played by the legendary horror movie star and original Frankenstein monster Boris Karloff.

PROFILE: **LERNER & LOEWE**

Alan Jay Lerner
Born: 31 August 1918, New York City
Died: 14 June 1986, New York City

Frederick Loewe
Born: 10 June 1901, Berlin, Germany
Died: 14 February 1988, Palm Springs, Florida

Major Shows: Brigadoon (1947), Paint Your Wagon (1951), My Fair Lady (1956), Camelot (1960)

Major Films: Brigadoon (1955), Gigi (1958), My Fair Lady (1964), Camelot (1967), Paint Your Wagon (1969)

Memorable Songs: Almost Like Being In Love (1947), I Talk To The Trees (1951), On The Street Where You Live, I Could Have Danced All Night (1956), Gigi, Thank Heaven For Little Girls (1958), How To Handle A Woman (1960)

UP WEST

"West End" theatre is a popular term for London's "theatreland", rather in the same way that "Broadway" theatre applies to the whole theatre district in midtown Manhattan. The theatre district is located in the west end of the city centre, and

LONGEST WEST END RUNS

The totals for number of performances do not include
previews. West End shows generally play eight
performances a week, or about 416 performances per year.

These figures are as of October 31, 2004 unless
otherwise indicated. Shows marked with an asterisk (*)
are still running.

MUSICAL	RUN	YEAR	THEATRE
Cats	8,500+	1981	New London Theatre
*Les Miserables	7,558+	1984	Apollo, 2004/Queens
Starlight Express	7,406	1984	Apollo
*Blood Brothers	7,296+	1983	Phoenix
*Phantom of the Opera	6,912	1986	Her Majestys
Buddy	5,000(10/01)	1989	Victoria Palace, 1995 Strand
Miss Saigon	4,264	1989	Theatre Royal
Jesus Christ Superstar	3,358	1972	Palace
Me and My Girl *(revival)*	3,303	1985	Adelphi
Rocky Horror Show	2,958	1973	Royal Court
Evita	2,900	1978	Prince Edward
Oliver	2,618	1960	New Theatre
Sound of Music	2,385	1961	Palace
Oh Calcutta	2,305+	1974	Royalty
Salad Days	2,329	1954	Vaudeville
My Fair Lady	2,281	1958	Theatre Royal
Chu Chin Chow	2,238	1916	His Majestys
Charlie Girl	2,202	1965	Adelphi
*Lion King	2,080+	1999	Royal Lyceum
The Boyfriend	2,084	1953	Wyndhams

is usually considered to be bordered by The Strand in the south, Oxford Street to the north, Regent Street to the west, and Kingsway to the east – although the South Bank complex on the other side of the River Thames is now often referred to as part of it. The main theatre streets include Drury Lane, Shaftesbury Avenue, and The Strand, and there are about forty large thetres in the district as a whole.

Most of the West End theatres are of late Victorian and Edwardian orgin, dating from the late 19th and early 20th century. Consequently they are generally splendid in character, the main down-side being often cramped leg room – people tended to be smaller a hundred years ago!

Although the theatres also present straight drama and comedy shows, musicals predominate both in popularity and longevity. The longest running musical in West End history was Andrew Lloyd Webber's *Cats*, which closed in 2001 after running for 9,000 performances, and the longest running current musical is *Les Misérables*. Having said that, the world record for longest-running show is held by the non-musical Agatha Christie play *The Mousetrap*, which has been playing since 1953.

STRICTLY BRITISH

Not all London successes have been taken up at the time by Broadway – or vice versa for that matter. These are some productions that ran for over a year in the West End without subsequently crossing the Atlantic.

SHOW / WRITERS / DATE / LONDON RUN
The Dancing Years Ivor Novello 1939 1156
Bless The Bride Herbert / Ellis 1947 886
King's Rhapsody Ivor Novello 1949 839

Free As Air Slade / Reynolds 1957 417
Blitz Lionel Bart 1962 568
Robert and Elizabeth Millar / Grainer 1964 948
Charlie Girl Heneker / Taylor 1965 2202

The biggest cross-over successes from London to New York have undoubtedly been the musicals of Andrew Lloyd Webber, with *Cats* clocking up 7485 performances and topping the list of all Broadway runs, followed closely by *The Phantom of the Opera* at over 7301 and still running.

A very English – indeed very London – musical arrived in the work of Lionel Bart. From the city's working class East End, he's been writing pop hits of UK rock idol Tommy Steele before bursting onto the theatre scene with *Fings Ain't What They Used To Be*, full of brash "cor blimey" exhubrance, with a book written by an ex-convict Frank Norman.

Bart had further success with *Oliver!* in 1960, which was a hit internationally and ran to 2618 performances in the West End. It was the longest-running British musical on Broadway up to that time, and Bart won a Tony award (Broadway's "Oscar") for the songs. It also went on to be a blockbuster film musical in 1968, directed by Carol Reed and starring Harry Secombe, Ron Moody and Shani Wallis with Mark Lester in the title role.

"If I'd known I was going to live this long, I'd have taken better care of myself. "
Pianist/composer Eubie Blake,
who died aged 96 in 1983

WEST END DIVAS

Many names have come and gone on the West End musical scene, performers who starred in London productions of home-grown and Broadway shows – and sometimes in America too – but often achieved a bigger name for themselves in other branches of show business.

Georgia Brown (b.1933, d.1992)
Shows: The Threepenny Opera, Oliver! (also in US), Carmelina (US), Maggie May. Also known as a jazz singer.

Fenella Fielding (b.1934)
Shows: Jubilee Girl, Valmouth, High Spirits
Better known as a film and TV character actress.

Shani Wallis (b.1938)
Shows: Call Me Madam, Wonderful Town, Finian's Rainbow, Irma La Douce, South Pacific (US), The King and I (US), 42nd Street (US) **Film:** Oliver! Also known as a cabaret performer.

Rachel Roberts (b.1927, d.1980)
Shows: The Buccaneer, Oh, My Papa! Maggie May. Better known as a straight actress.

Eleanor Summerfield (b.1921, d.2001)
Shows: Golden City, When in Rome. Better known as a film actress.

Patricia Routledge (b.1929)
Shows: Little Mary Sunshine, Darling of the Day (US), Love Match (US), 1600 Pennsylvania Avenue (US), Carousel
Better known as a TV character actress.

In many ways the crowning moment of the era of the classic musical came with *West Side Story* which opened on Broadway in 1958. It was the ultimate "story" vehicle, adapted from Shakespeare's *Romeo and Juliet*, and the perfect blend of song, dance and drama. Leonard Bernstein's score incorporated classical and jazz influences, and every single song was memorable. And at the same time, it heralded a new style of musical with a grittier, more socially realistic edge.

> *"To achieve great things, two things are needed;*
> *a plan, and not quite enough time. "*
> Leonard Bernstein

LEGENDARY MUSICALS:
WEST SIDE STORY

New York's Hell's Kitchen was the setting for the eventually tragic story of Tony and Maria, lovers from across the racial divide perpetuated by white and Puerto Rican street gangs, the Jets and the Sharks.

Lyrics: Stephen Sondheim
Music: Leonard Bernstein
Book: Arthur Laurents, based on Shakespeare's *Romeo and Juliet* from an idea by Jerome Robbins

First Performance:
New York, 26 September 1957, Winter Gardens Theater (734 performances)
London, 12 December 1958, Her Majesty's Theater, (1039 performances)

Hit songs: *'Jet Song', 'Tonight, 'Maria, 'America', 'Something's Coming', 'I Feel Pretty', 'Somewhere', 'Gee Officer Krupke!'*

Film version: 1961 (Natalie Wood, Richard Beymer. Directors, Robert Wise / Jerome Robbins)

"I'm not interested in having an orchestra sound like itself.
I want it to sound like the composer."
Leonard Bernstein

PROFILE: **GEORGE AND IRA GERSHWIN**

George Gershwin
Born: Jacob Gershovitz, 26 September 1898, New York City
Died: 11 June 1937, Los Angeles

Ira Gershwin
Born: Israel Gershovitz, 6 December 1896, New York City
Died: 17 August 1983, Los Angeles

Major Shows: Lady Be Good (1924), Funny Face (1927), Porgy and Bess (1935)

Major Films: Shall We Dance? (1937), Porgy and Bess (1959)

Memorable Songs: Lady Be Good, The Man I Love, Fascinating Rhythm (1924), Someone To Watch Over Me (1926), S'Wonderful (1927), I Got Rhythm, Embraceable You, But Not For Me (1930), It Aint Necessarily So, Summertime (1935), Let's Call The Whole Thing Off, They Can't Take That Away From Me, A Foggy Day (1937)

"Why should I limit myself to only one woman when I can have as many women as I want?"
George Gershwin

"A song without music is a lot like H2 without the O."
Ira Gershwin

The Gershwins' *Porgy and Bess* was not strictly a musical, but a fully fledged opera   – often acclaimed as the first great American opera – and was actually a flop when it first ran on Broadway in 1935. Not received well by critics, it closed after just 124 performances, losing all its backers' money. But a 1942 revival, which this time had the reviewers raving, ran longer than any revival in the history of US musical theatre. A US State Department-sponsored tour in 1952 took the all-black production on a four-year world tour of 29 countries, including the USSR. It was the first American opera to be seen at La Scala, Milan, and in 1959 a spectacular film was released with Sidney Poitier, Dorothy Dandridge, Sammy Davis Jnr, Pearl Bailey and Diahann Carroll.

> *"Critics complained it wasn't opera, it wasn't a musical.*
> *You give someone something delicious to eat and they complain*
> *because they have no name for it."*
> Rouben Mamoulian, on *Porgy and Bess*

Carmen Jones, a 1943 all-black stage adaptation of Bizet's opera *Carmen* with lyrics by Oscar Hammerstein II, was filmed in 1954 by Otto Preminger, who went on to direct *Porgy and Bess*. The cast included Dorothy Dandridge, Pearl Bailey and Diahann Carroll who would all later appear in *Porgy'*, plus Harry Belafonte in the lead.

Opera Adaptations

A number of musicals have been based on, or inspired by, classic operas.

MUSICAL / YEAR / BASED ON / COMPOSER
Once Over Lightly 1942 The Barber of Seville *Rossini*
Carmen Jones 1943 Carmen *Bizet*
My Darlin' Aida 1952 Aida *Verdi*
Miss Saigon 1992 Madame Butterfly *Puccini*
Rent 1996 La Bohème *Puccini*

WHERE'S THAT SONG FROM?

Most of the so-called "standards", the songs that are
familiar to all and always seem to have been around, have
their roots in stage musicals. Here are just twenty such
classics that have lasted long after the shows they
came from are all but forgotten.

SONG / (COMPOSER) / SHOW / YEAR

Manhattan (Rodgers/Hart) Garrick Gaieties 1925

Someone To Watch Over Me (Gershwin) Oh Kay! 1926

Mountain Greenery (Rodgers/Hart) The Girl Friend 1927

How Long Has This Been Going On (Gershwin) Rosalie 1928

Love Me Or Leave Me (Kahn/Donaldson) Whoopee 1928

Makin' Whoopee (Kahn/Donaldson) Whoopee 1928

My Baby Just Cares For Me (Kahn/Donaldson) Whoopee 1928

With A Song In My Heart (Rodgers/Hart) Spring Is Here 1929

I Got Rhythm (Gershwin) Girl Crazy 1930

Love For Sale (Porter) The New Yorkers 1930

Night And Day (Porter) The Gay Divorce 1932

You're The Top (Porter) Anything Goes 1934

Just One Of Those Things (Porter) Jubilee 1935

It's De-Lovely (Porter) Red, Hot And Blue 1936

I Didn't Know What Time It Was (Rodgers/Hart)
Too Many Girls 1939

The Lady Is A Tramp (Rodgers/Hart) Babes In Arms 1939

I Wish I Were In Love Again (Rodgers/Hart) Babes In Arms 1939

My Funny Valentine (Rodgers/Hart) Babes In Arms 1939

Come Rain Or Come Shine (Mercer/Arlen) St Louis Woman 1946

From This Moment On (Porter) Out of This World 1950

HOLLYWOOD HIGHS

The roots of the movie musical go back to 1927 and the very beginning of the sound era, when, in the first-ever "talkie" *The Jazz Singer*, Al Jolson sang songs like 'Toot Toot Tootsie', 'My Mammy' and 'Blue Skies' (none of which had anything to do with jazz). It was otherwise a silent picture – except for some additional snatches of dialogue, including Jolson's famous exclamation "You ain't heard nothin' yet!"

The Jazz Singer was remade twice. Warner Brothers tackled it in 1953 with Danny Thomas and Peggy Lee starring, and a third version appeared in 1980 with Neil Diamond and – somewhat bizarrely – Sir Laurence Olivier.

Many of the earliest screen musicals were glorified stage reviews with no plot to speak of. The titles, like *Paramount On Parade*, *Broadway Melody* and *Golddiggers of Broadway* said it all, but they did enable Hollywood to exploit film technology in spectacular sets and ambitious production numbers that were impossible to achieve in the theatre.

It soon became apparent that cinema audiences wanted more than a two-dimensional (and black-and-white) version of Vaudeville, so the next step was adaptations of established stage hits like *The Desert Song* (1929), *Rio Rita* (1929) and *The Vagabond King* (1930).

Very soon the film industry was originating its own musicals. Early Hollywood-born successes included the vehicles for the song and dance team of Fred Astaire and Ginger Rogers, like *Top Hat* (1935) and *Follow the Fleet* (1936), both directed by Mark Sandrich and with songs by Irving Berlin.

PROFILE: FRED ASTAIRE

Born: Frederick Austerlitz, 10 May 1899, Omaha, Nebraska
Died: 22 June 1987, Los Angeles

Major Films: Flying Down To Rio (1933), Top Hat (1935), Follow the Fleet (1936), Holiday Inn (1942), Ziegfeld Follies (1946), Easter Parade (1948), Three Little Words (1950), The Band Wagon (1953), Daddy Long Legs (1955), Funny Face, Sik Stockings (1957), Finian's Rainbow (1958)

Hit Songs: 'Lady be Good', 'Fascinating Rhythm', 'Dancing In The Dark', 'Night And Day', 'The Way You Look Tonight', 'I Won't Dance', 'They Can't Take That Away From Me', 'A Foggy Day', 'A Fine Romance'

A graduate of the Broadway stage, song and dance director Busby Berkeley forged a choreographic style unique to the cinema. Starting with Warner Brothers' *42nd Street* in 1933, he staged spectacular musical numbers involving scores of chorus girls in complicated kaleioscopic patterns, often shot from seemingly impossible angles. He had a habit of cutting a hole in the studio roof just to get the right overhead shot, and the amazing results adorned Thirties musicals like *Gold Diggers of 1933*, *Footlight Parade* and *Stage Struck*. In the Fifties he directed the famous water ballets for aqua-star Esther Williams in *Million Dollar Mermaid* (1952) and 1953's *Easy to Love*.

Biographical films of famous songwriters became a popular Hollywood vehicle to run through some of the best songs ever written, featuring the particular studios' own musical stars. With storylines more in the realm of fiction than fact, most of the great popular composers of the 20th centuy were celebrated in this way.

YEAR / FILM / COMPOSER / STARRING

1945 **Rhapsody In Blue** George Gershwin
Robert Alda
1945 **Night and Day** Cole Porter
Cary Grant
1946 **Till the Clouds Roll By** Jerome Kern
Robert Walker
1948 **Words and Music** Rodgers & Hart
Tom Drake, Mickey Rooney

Conceived as a perfect showcase for its roster of contracted music names, MGM's 1948 Rodgers and Hart biopic *Words and Music* featured a number of stars in cameo roles playing themselves, including Judy Garland, June Allyson, Gene Kelly, Lena Horne, Mel Tormé and Vera-Ellen. Other big names in the production, playing fictional roles, were crooner Perry Como, dancer Cyd Charisse and actress/singer Betty Garrett.

Other musical biographies dealing with the musical stage of Vaudeville and Broadway have included

YEAR / FILM / STARRING / SUBJECT

1936 **The Great Ziegfeld** William Powell
Impressario Florenz Ziegfeld
1942 **Yankee Doodle Dandy** James Cagney
Vaudevillian George M. Cohan
1955 **The Seven Little Foys** Bob Hope
Vaudeville entertainer Eddie Foy
1955 **Love Me or Leave Me** Doris Day
Singer Ruth Etting

With the advent of the "story" musical in the Forties it became far easier to transfer productions to the silver screen without radically changing, or adding to, the nararrative plot. This reached boom proportions in the Fifites with block-buster versions of the great Rodgers and Hammerstein shows like *Oklahoma, Carousel, The King And I,* and most successful of all at the time, *South Pacific.* And in the following decade, this was topped by the unprecedented popularity of *The Sound of Music,* the Julie Andrews movie which has remained a cult item to this day.

Many other Broadway productions found an audience in cinemas all over the world. These included Rodgers and Hart's *A Connecticut Yankee*, filmed in 1948 and starring Bing Crosby, and the seminal Leonard Bernstein-scored *On The Town*, a spectacular stage show in 1943 but even more historic movie in 1949.

The movie of *On The Town*, largely shot on location in New York, was important in that it was the official directorial debut of Stanley Donen and his first collaboration with dancer-director Gene Kelly. The two went on to work together on several more films, including *Singin' In The Rain* in 1952, *Deep in My Heart* (1954) and *It's Always Fair Weather* ('55).

Other classic Broadway shows that made significant motion pictures in the Fifties included Cole Porter's *Kiss Me Kate* (1953), Lerner and Loewe's *Brigadoon* and Sigmund Romberg's operetta *The Student Prince* (both in 1954), Frank Loesser's marvellous take on Damon Runyon's New York stories, *Guys and Dolls* (1955), Rodgers and Hart's *Pal Joey* (1957) and Cole Porter's *Can-Can* (released in 1960).

FOUR CLASSIC HOLLYWOOD ADAPTATIONS

Kiss Me Kate (1953) MGM
Directed: George Sidney
Original Stage Production: 1948
Music by: Cole Porter
Starring: Howard Keel, Kathryn Grayson, Ann Miller
Hit songs: 'Wunderbar', 'So In Love', 'Always True To You In My Fashion', 'Brush Up Your Shakespeare'

Guys And Dolls (1955) Samuel Goldwyn
Directed: Joseph Mankiewicz
Original Stage Production: 1950
Music by: Frank Loesser
Starring: Marlon Brando, Frank Sinatra, Jean Simmons
Hit songs: 'Adelaide', 'Luck Be A Lady', 'Sit Down You're Rockin' The Boat', 'A Woman In Love'

The King and I (1956) 20th Century Fox
Directed: Walter Lang
Original Stage Production: 1951
Music by: Rodgers and Hammerstein
Starring: Deborah Kerr, Yul Brynner
Hit songs: 'Hello Young Lovers', 'Getting To Know You', 'Shall We Dance' 'Whistle A Happy Tune'

The Sound of Music (1965) 20th Century Fox
Directed: Robert Wise
Original Stage Production: 1959
Music by: Rodgers and Hammerstein
Starring: Julie Andrews, Christopher Plummer
Hit songs: 'The Sound Of Music', 'Favourite Things', 'Do-Re-Mi', 'Climb Every Mountain', 'Edelweiss'

WHO SANG THAT?

Many singing parts on classic film musicals have been dubbed by other people, particularly when actors couldn't sing adequetly or (in the case of the overweight Mario Lanza in *The Student Prince*) if the singer simply didn't look the part.

FILM / ACTOR / SINGER
My Fair Lady
Audrey Hepburn – Marni Nixon

Pal Joey
Rita Hayworth – Jo Ann Greer, Kim Novak – Trudy Erwin

South Pacific
Rossano Brazzi – Giorgio Tozzi, John Kerr – Bill Lee
Juanita Hall – Muriel Smith

The Student Prince
Edmund Purdom – Mario Lanza

West Side Story
Natalie Wood – Marni Nixon, Richard Beymer – Jim Bryant
Rita Moreno – Betty Wand

The radical changeover that Hollywood underwent with the introduction of sound was brilliantly highlighted in *Singin' In The Rain*, one of the all-time favourite musicals to originate as a movie, which was made in 1952. Starring Gene Kelly, Debbie Reynolds and Donald O'Connor, it represented a high point in the golden age of the film musical at MGM studios, with songs that included 'Make Em' Laugh', 'You Were Meant For Me', 'Good Morning', 'All I Do Is Dream Of You' and of course the memorable title number. Most of the songs were by Arthur Freed and Nacio Herb Brown, and were actually written for earlier MGM musicals.

Singin' In The Rain was adapted for the West End stage in 1983, and starring Tommy Steele (who also directed) it also included several new songs. It ran for over three years, breaking all records at the London Palladium, although a 1985 Broadway production failed to even cover its costs. The latter was one of several examples of adaptations of movie musicals to the stage being far less successful than the reverse, the most famous example being a 1982 stage version of *Seven Brides For Seven Brothers*, which closed after just five performances in New York.

········ MADE FOR THE MOVIES ········

The escapist Fred Astaire and Busby Berkeley musicals of the Thirties led the way, and after World War II Hollywood produced a wealth of original musicals. The War itself paved the way, when patriotic morale-boosting films like MGM's *Thousands Cheer* and Paramount's *Star-Spangled Rhythm* were typical of what was coming out of all the big studios.

After the War new names emerged on the studios' musical rosters, such as Doris Day, Howard Keel and Frank Sinatra. Doris Day in particular made mainly Hollywood-originated musicals, often light romantic comedies like *On Moonlight Bay* (1951), *April In Paris* (1952) and *Young At Heart* (with Sinatra, 1954). But her *tour de force* came in the dynamic 1953 western musical *Calamity Jane*, in which her co-star (as Wild Bill Hickock) was Howard Keel.

FOUR CLASSIC HOLLYWOOD ORIGINALS

An American In Paris (1951) MGM
Directed: Vincente Minnelli
Music by: George & Ira Gershwin
Starring: Gene Kelly, Leslie Caron

Hit songs: 'I Got Rhythm', 'Embraceable You', 'Our Love Is Here To Stay'

Singin' In The Rain (1952) MGM
Directed: Stanley Donen / Gene Kelly
Music by: Arthur Freed / Nacio Herb Brown
Starring: Gene Kelly, Debbie Reynolds, Donald O'Connor
Hit songs: 'You Were Meant For Me', 'Good Morning', 'All I Do Is Dream Of You', 'Singin' In The Rain'

Calamity Jane (1953) Warner Brothers
Directed: David Butler
Music by: Sammy Fain / Paul Francis Webster
Starring: Doris Day, Howard Keel
Hit songs: 'Secret Love', 'The Deadwood Stage', 'The Black Hills Of Dakota'

Seven Brides For Seven Brothers (1954) MGM
Directed: Stanley Donen
Music by: Johnny Mercer / Jean de Paul
Starring: Howard Keel, Jane Powell
Hit songs: 'Spring Spring Spring', 'Bless Your Beautiful Hide', 'Goin Co'tin'

"I think you should make more movies, more musicals.
I think the public deserves that. I think this country deserves to be able to
get out and foster that talent. Give them an opportunity to become stars.
I think the whole idea is wonderful. "
Donald O'Connor

Three creative powerhouses took the movie musical to new artistic heights. They were choreographer / directors Stanley Donen and Gene Kelly (who collaborated several times) and the director Vincente Minnelli. Donen and Kelly worked together on two landmark Hollywood musicals – *On The Town* (though not an actual movie original) and *Singin' In The Rain*. Minnelli and Kelly were responsible for the oft-underrated *The*

Pirate in 1948, and the director's 1951 masterpiece *An American In Paris*, which ranks alongside *Singin' In The Rain* as the Hollywood-generated musical at its peak.

PROFILE: **GENE KELLY**

Born: Eugene Curran Kelly, 23 August 1912, Pittsburgh, Pennsylvania
Died: 1 February 1996, Los Angeles

Major Films: Anchors Aweigh (1945), The Pirate (1948), On The Town (1949), An American In Paris (1951), Singin' In The Rain (1952), Brigadoon, Deep In My Heart 1954), It's Always Fair Weather (1955)

Hit Songs: 'New York, New York', 'Singin' In The Rain', 'You Were Meant For Me', 'S'Wonderful', 'I Got Rhythm', 'Almost Like Being In Love'

BOX OFFICE BONANZAS

Bearing in mind the relatively low level of cinema ticket prices forty or more years ago, the phenomenal success of *The Sound of Music* – and another Julie Andrews smash hit *Mary Poppins* – is illustrated in the list of the all-time biggest grossing movie musicals at the US box office.

Chicago $170,684,505 (2002)
The Sound of Music $163,214,286 (1965)
Doctor Dolittle $144,156,464 (1998)
The Rocky Horror Picture Show $139,876,417 (1975)
Mary Poppins $102,300,000 (1964)

Although the golden age can be dated from 1949's
On the Town to *The Sound of Music* in 1965,
there have been some memorable movie musicals since.
Here are a dozen of the best, including (in parenthesis)
the date of the original stage show, songwriters,
director and stars.

Annie 1982 (1976)
Songs: Martin Charnin, Charles Strauss
Directed: John Huston
Starring: Aileen Quinn, Albert Finney

Best Little Whorehouse In Texas 1982 (1977)
Songs: Carol Hall
Directed: Colin Higgins
Starring: Dolly Parton, Burt Reynolds

Cabaret 1972 (1966)
Songs: Fred Ebb, John Kander
Directed: Bob Fosse
Starring: Liza Minnelli, Michael York

Chicago 2002 (1975)
Songs: Fred Ebb, John Kander
Directed: Rob Marshall
Starring: Catherine Zeta-Jones, Renée Zellweger,
Richard Gere

A Chorus Line 1985 (1975)
Songs: Marvin Hamlisch & Edward Kleban
Directed: Alan Parker
Starring: Madonna, Jonathan Pryce

Evita 1996 (1978)
Songs: Tim Rice, Andrew Lloyd Webber
Directed: Alan Parker
Starring: Madonna, Jonathan Pryce
Godspell 1973 (1971)
Songs: Stephen Schwartz
Directed: David Greene
Starring: Victor Garber, David Haskell

Jesus Christ Superstar 1973 (1971)
Songs: Tim Rice, Andrew Lloyd Webber
Directed: Norman Jewison
Starring: Ted Neely, Carl Anderson

Little Shop of Horrors 1986 (1982)
Songs: Howard Ashman, Alan Menken
Directed: Frank Oz
Starring: Ellen Greene, Rick Moranis

The Phantom of the Opera 2004 (1986)
Songs: Charles Hart, Andrew Lloyd Webber
Directed: Joel Schumacher
Starring: Gerard Butler, Emmy Rossum

Rent 2005 (1996)
Songs: Jonathan Larson
Directed: Chris Columbus
Starring: Rosario Dawson, Taye Diggs

The Rocky Horror Picture Show 1975 (1973)
Songs: Richard O'Brian
Directed: Jim Sharman
Starring: Tim Curry, Susan Sarandon

OSCAR SONGS

**While the Best Song category at the annual
Academy Awards has often been won for songs
featured in otherwise non-musical films, here
are the songs from movie musicals
(or music-oriented films) that grabbed the Oscar.**

BEST SONG ACADEMY AWARD WINNERS

1934 The Continental *The Gay Divorcee*

1935 Lullaby of Broadway *Gold Diggers of 1935*

1936 The Way You Look Tonight *Swing Time*

1937 Sweet Leilani *Waikiki Wedding*

1938 Thanks for the Memory *Big Broadcast of 1938*

1939 Over the Rainbow *The Wizard of Oz*

1941 The Last Time I Saw Paris *Lady Be Good*

1942 White Christmas *Holiday Inn*

1943 You'll Never Know *Hello, Frisco, Hello*

1944 Swinging on a Star *Going My Way*

1945 It Might As Well Be Spring *State Fair*

1946 On the Atchison, Topeka and the Santa Fe
The Harvey Girls

1947 Zip-A-Dee-Doo-Dah *Song of the South*

1948 Buttons and Bows *The Paleface*

1949 Baby, It's Cold Outside *Neptune's Daughter*

1951 In the Cool, Cool, Cool of the Evening
Here Comes the Groom

1953 Secret Love *Calamity Jane*

1958 Gigi *Gigi*
1964 Chim Chim Cheree *Mary Poppins*
1967 Talk to the Animals *Doctor Dolittle*
1976 Evergreen *A Star Is Born*
1994 Can You Feel the Love Tonight *The Lion King*
1996 You Must Love Me *Evita*

Oscar Winners

The Sixties saw most Academy Award-winning
musicals for Best Picture.

Year / Film / Director

1929 **Broadway Melody** Harry Beaumont
1958 **Gigi** Vincente Minnelli
1961 **West Side Story** Jerome Robbins, Robert Wise
1964 **My Fair Lady** George Cukor
1965 **The Sound of Music** Robert Wise
1968 **Oliver!** Carol Reed
2002 **Chicago** Rob Marshall

*"Musicals became too expensive. When we were working at
MGM, there was a whole company of talent - stars, directors,
choreographers, song writers, conductors, arrangers.
All worked under contract at regular salaries. To gather people
like that today would be enormously costly."*
George Sidney

REEL BRITANNIA

Although rarely as high profile as its Hollywood counterpart, the British cinema has produced some memorable musicals over the years. In the Thirties it was the launch pad for huge domestic stars like Gracie Fields and George Formby, as well as eventual exports to Hollywood including the suave song and dance man Jack Buchanan.

The Forties and Fifties saw romantic extravaganzas on a grand scale, while what was considered the first "Hollywood" style musical to come in post-war British movies came with the Cliff Richard vehicle *The Young Ones* in 1961. Through the swingin' Sixties there were many pop films which weren't musicals as such, the best of which was The Beatles' *A Hard Days Night*, but the more traditional movie musical continued to be represented in works like *Oliver!* and Ken Russell's *The Boyfriend*.

Many famous directors have been at the helm of British musicals, from Herbert Wilcox and Val Guest through Michael Winner (*The Cool Mikado*) and Carol Reed (*Oliver!*) to Alan Parker with *Bugsy Malone* and Baz Luhrmann's Anglo-Australian spectacular *Moulin Rouge*.

BRITISH MOVIE MUSICALS – TWENTY OF THE BEST

1931 **Man of Mayfair** with Jack Buchanan. **Director**: Louis Mercanton

1931 **Sally in Our Alley** with Gracie Fields, Florence Desmond. **Director:** Maurice Elvey

1934 **Boots, Boots** with George Formby, Betty Driver. **Director:** Bert Tracy

1934 **Chu Chin Chow** with Anna May Wong, George Robey.
Director: Walter Forde

1944 **Champagne Charlie** with Tommy Trinder, Stanley
Holloway **Director:** Alberto Cavalcanti

1945 **Waltz Time** with Richard Tauber, Peter Graves, Patricia
Medina, Kay Kendall, Anne Ziegler and Webster Booth.
Director: Paul L. Stein

1955 **King's Rhapsody** with Errol Flynn, Patrice Wymore, Anna
Neagle **Director:** Herbert Wilcox

1959 **Expresso Bongo** with Laurence Harvey, Sylvia Syms, Cliff
Richard **Director:** Val Guest

1961 **The Young Ones** with Cliff Richard, The Shadows,
Melvyn Hayes **Director:** Sidney J. Furie

1963 **The Cool Mikado** with Frankie Howerd, Janet Blair,
Stubby Kaye **Director:** Michael Winner

1963 **What a Crazy World** with Joe Brown, Harry H. Corbett,
Avis Bunnage **Director:** Michael Carreras

1966 **Stop the World, I Want to Get Off** with Tony Tanner,
Millicent Martin **Director:** Philip Saville

1967 **Half a Sixpence** with Tommy Steele, Julia Foster
Director: George Sidney

1968 **Chitty Chitty Bang Bang** with Dick Van Dyke, Sally Ann
Howes **Director:** Ken Hughes

1968 **Oliver!** with Mark Lester, Ron Moody, Harry Secombe,
Shani Wallis **Director:** Carol Reed

1971 **The Boy Friend** with Twiggy, Christopher Gable, Tommy Tune **Director:** Ken Russell

1975 **The Rocky Horror Picture Show** with Tim Curry, Susan Sarandon **Director**: Jim Sharman

1976 **Bugsy Malone** with Scott Baio, Jodie Foster **Director:** Alan Parker

1986 **Absolute Beginners** with Eddie O'Connell, Patsy Kensit, David Bowie **Director:** Julien Temple

2001 **Moulin Rouge** with Nicole Kidman, Ewan McGregor **Director:** Baz Luhrmann

Despite making Gracie Fields a star and giving her a signature tune, *Sally In Our Alley* (1931) – set in working class Britain – didn't have the same resonance in the United States, where *Variety* magazine commented "The songs are just numbers, the general standard nothing to shout about "

Written by children's author Roald Dahl from a novel by James Bond creator Ian Flemming, 1968's *Chitty Chitty Bang Bang* went on to be a hugely successful West End musical, clocking up 1,456 performances at the London Palladium from the 2003 opening to its closing in September 2005. It also enjoys a continuing Broadway run, opening at the Hilton The   n April 2005.

After much balyhoo as being the new breakthrough in British musical cinema, Julian Temple's 1986 adaptation of the seminal Fifties novel *Absolute Beginners* by Colin MacInnes was judged by most critics as an absolute disaster – despite the presence of James Fox and Steven Berkoff, plus rock stars David Bowie and the Kinks' Ray Davies in singing and acting roles.

DEDICATED TO YOU

The compilation musical, a near-relative of the traditional revue, is either a celebration of a particular theme (jazz of the Thirties and Forties in *All Night Strut* (1979), songs of wartime Britain in *Happy as a Sandbag* (1975) and so on), or the works of a particular artist. In the latter category, many names have been celebrated in this way. We're not talking about semi-biographical shows like the Buddy Holly musical *Buddy*, but presentations of a selection of songs as a tribute vehicle – and an entertaining show.

SHOW / YEAR / CELEBRATING THE WORK OF…

Ain't Misbehavin' 1978 Singer/composer Fats Waller

Berlin To Broadway 1972 German songwriter Kurt Weill

Cowardy Custard 1972 Playwrite /composer Noel Coward

Decline and Fall of the Entire World As Seen Through the Eyes of Cole Porter 1965 Songwriter Cole Porter

Eubie! 1978 Composer/pianist Eubie Blake

It's a Grand Night for Singing 1993 Songwriters Rodgers & Hammerstein

Jacques Brel Is Alive and Well and Living In Paris 1966 French singer/writer Jacques Brel

Jerry's Girls 1985 Songwriter Jerry Herman

Perfectly Frank 1980 Songwriter Frank Loesser

Side By Side By Sondheim 1976 Songwriter Stephen Sondheim

Sing For Your Supper 1975 Songwriters Rodgers & Hart

Some Enchanted Evening 1983 Songwriters Rodgers & Hammerstein

Sophisticated Ladies 1981 Musician/Songwriter Duke Ellington

Swell Party 1991 Songwriter Cole Porter

Tomfoolery 1980 Satirical songwriter Tom Lehrer

Underneath the Arches 1982 British song / comedy duo Flanagan and Allen

You're Gonna Love Tomorrow 1983 Songwriter Stephen Sondheim.

THE MODERN MUSICAL

···· A NEW REALISM ····

In the wake of *West Side Story* the musical opened up in terms of subject matter, with more "realistic" storylines often addressing social issiues. The traditional formula of romantic themes and song-and-dance escapism still survived of course, as evidenced in the success of shows like *The Sound of Music* and *Mame*, but 1958's *Irma-la-Douce* (about a Parisien prostitute) and *Fiddler On The Roof* (1964, set against Jewish persecution in Tzarist Russia) were just as much the order of the day.

When *Irma-la-Douce* opened in London in 1958 it ran for more performances than its French original. Along with the more recent *Les Miserables*, it was one of the few musicals from Continental Europe to make an impact worldwide. After playing Broadway for over a year from September 1960, in 1963 a non-musical film was released starring Shirley McLean and Jack Lemmon, directed by the great Billy Wilder.

Working class London had been the setting for Lionel Bart's first foray into the West End in 1959 with *Fings Ain't Wot They Used T'Be*, and he followed through (after his huge success with *Oliver!* in 1960) with a musical set in the war-torn East End, *Blitz!* In 1964 (undoubtedly responding to trends in the world of pop music) he shifted his spotlight to the docklands of Liverpool for *Maggie May*, about a streetwalker and her trade unionist boyfriend.

YEAR / SHOW / SUBJECT AND SETTING
1958 **Irma-la-Douce** Story of a Parisien prostitute
1958 **Expresso Bongo** Satirical exposé of pop music scene
1959 **Fiorello!** Biography of New York mayor La Guardia
1960 **Tederloin** New York's 19th century red light district
1961 **Belle** Mass-murderer Doctor Crippen
1962 **Blitz!** London's East End during World War II
1963 **Oh What A Lovely War!** Anti-war satire
1964 **Maggie May** Liverpool dockland saga
1966 **Cabaret** Rise of Nazis in pre-war Berlin
1967 **Annie** The Depression and Roosevelt's New Deal

PROFILE: **LIONEL BART**

Born: Lionel Begleiter, 1 August 1930, London
Died: 3 April 1999, London

Major Shows: Fings Ain't Wot They Used T'Be (1959), Oliver! (1960), Blitz! (1962), Maggie May (1964)

Major Films: Oliver! (1968)

Memorable Songs: Living Doll, Fings Ain't Wot They Used T'Be (1959), Consider Yourself, Food Glorious Food, As Long As He Needs Me (1960)

"Lionel (Bart) was the father of the modern British musical.
As composer, book writer and lyricist of Oliver! he was responsible for one
of the greatest musicals of all time and ... he wrote arguably the
all-time perfect pop song, 'Living Doll'"
Andrew Lloyd Webber

THE ROCK MUSICAL

When *Hair* opened on Broadway in 1968 it was hailed as the first ever rock musical. With a plot concerning drug-taking draft-dodging hippies at the time of the Vietnam War, it was very much of its era. Even the songs, with titles like 'Aquarius', 'Good Morning Starshine', 'Hare Krishna' and 'Let The Sunshine In', have dated far faster than tunes from decades earlier.

Hair's first New York run of 1750 at the Biltmore Theater (taking over $7million in just over two years) was surpassed in the West End, where a total of 2,000 shows was thwarted when the theatre roof collapsed after the 1999th performance!

There had been musicals *about* rock music of course. The most successful of these was *Bye Bye Birdie*, a 1960 Broadway satire inspired by the drafting of Elvis Presley into the US Army. Similarly, the UK's *Expresso Bongo* in 1958 was a spoof on the stereotypical dumb rock singer and fast-talking manager. Both musicals made it to the screen, *'Bongo* in 1959 with Cliff Richard and Laurence Harvey, and *'Birdie* in 1963 starring Ann-Margret and Bobby Rydell.

1958's musical satire on the early rock'n'roll business, *Expresso Bongo*, starred real-life pop star Tommy Steele – the UK's very first rock idol – in its first London run. Steele went on to even bigger West End success with the 1963 musical *Half A Sixpence* (based on H.G. Wells' novel *Kipps*), written by *'Bongo* composer David Heneker. The movie of *Expresso Bongo*, meanwhile, starred Steele's biggest rival as Britain's No 1 rocker, Cliff Richard.

The success of *Hair* triggered a fashion for rock musicals in the early Seventies. These ranged from the highly successful *Jesus*

Christ Superstar and *Godspell* to spectacular flops. The latter included *Dude*, which folded in 1972 after 16 shows, and *Via Galactica* the same year, which with just eight performances to its credit was one of the first Broadway musicals to lose more than a million dollars.

Jesus Christ Superstar, which opened in 1971, heralded the arrival on the scene of Tim Rice and Andrew Lloyd Webber. It ran for 711 performances on Broadway, but its London run which started in 1972 logged up an incredible 3358 shows. Until that figure was topped by Lloyd Webber's *Cats,* it held the record for the longest-running West End musical of all time.

Superstar was preceeded by a few months in New York by *Godspell,* which the American critics and audiences took to much more readily first time round. Also in 1971 audiences were treated to a multi-racial rock version of Shakespeare's *Two Gentlemen Of Verona,* followed the following year by the most successful of all rock musicals to to hit the Great White Way – *Grease.* The musical pastiche of Fifties rock'n'roll set in an archetypal American high school also memorably transferred to the screen with John Travolta and Olivia Newton-John in 1978.

VINTAGE ROCKERS

Hair (1967) **Songwriters:** Gerome Ragni, James Rado, Galt McDermot **1ˢᵗ US run:** 1566 **1ˢᵗ UK run** 1998 **Film:** 1979, directed Milos Forman

Godspell (1967) **Songwriters:** Gerome Ragni, James Rado, Galt McDermot
1ˢᵗ US run: 2751 **1ˢᵗ UK run** 1128 **Film:** 1979, directed Milos Forman

Jesus Christ Superstar (1971) **Songwriters:** Tim Rice, Andrew Lloyd Webber
1st US run: 711 **1st UK run** 3358 **Film:** 1973, directed Norman Jewison

Two Gentlemen of Verona (1971) **Songwriters:** John Guare, Mel Shapiro, Galt McDermot **1st US run:** 627

Grease (1972) **Songwriters:** Jim Jacobs, Warren Casey
1st US run: 3388 **1st UK run** 236 **Film:** 1978, directed Randal Kleiser

The Wiz (1975) **Songwriter:** Charlie Smalls
1st US run: 1672 **Film:** 1978, directed Sidney Lumet

The Wiz, which was a soul music version of *The Wizard Of Oz*, became a Motown-produced movie in 1978 starring Diana Ross and Michael Jackson.

A usually more pretentious version of the rock musical came with the "rock opera". Originally conceived on so-called concept albums like The Who's *Tommy* (1969) and *Quadrophenia* (1973), the first-ever full-length rock opera album was by The Pretty Things in 1968, *SF Sorrow*. But the first to be hugely successful was *Tommy*, which ended up being produced on the Broadway and West End stage, and as a big-budget movie.

The "progressive rock" era of the early Seventies was a heyday for the rock opera, though many never reached the stage and exist only as audio albums. Notable among these was *The Lamb Lies Down on Broadway* by prog-rock superstars Genesis in 1974, and David Bowie's *Diamond Dogs*, which was originally written as a rock opera version of George Orwell's *1984* until the Orwell estate denied Bowie permission to produce it.

In recent years, rock musicals have often taken the form of nothing more than reviews which have utilised existing songs in a thematic way. This has either been in a semi-biographical context, as with the Buddy Holly musical *Buddy* which was hugely successful in London from 1989 (with over 5,000 performances before the end of its 13-year run) or with songs linked (usually associated with one group or artist) by a plot. The latter device was used very successfully in *Mama Mia* (2001 and still running), based around the songs of Abba, and *We Will Rock You* (2002 and still running) which celebrated the music of Queen with a story set in a grim anti-fun future.

BIZARRO ROCK

Some rock operas, many of which never made it to the theatre stage, but worth listing on account of their unlikely subject matter!

Bonnie and Clyde   Musical based on the lives of the two American bank robbers and killers.

Buster Crabbe – The Rock Opera   Why they'd base a musical on the Thirties Flash Gordon star is hard to imagine.

Congregation Against Styrocultural Brain Damage Worth mentioning for the title!

Drakula the Rock Opera   Bram Stoker's *Dracula* originated by the Milwaukee Rock Opera Company and first performed in 1997.

Faust   Written by singer Randy Newman in 1995 and based on the novel by Goethe.

Galilei – Rock Opera By German and American composers, based on the life of Galileo.

Hunchback From 1998 when it opened in Seattle, based on Victor Hugo's *The Hunchback Of Notre Dame*.

In Spite of Reason Depicting the life of Abraham Lincoln during the Civil War.

Jack the Ripper Based on the case of the notorious London serial killer.

Macbeth – the Space Rock Opera A rock treatment of one of William Shakespeare's most bloodthirsty plays.

Zombie Prom Rejected by girlfriend, boy jumps into a nuclear power plant, then returns as a nuclear zombie to win back lost love.

THAT FOSSE TOUCH

Dancer and actor **Bob Fosse** was also one of America's greatest choreographers and directors, and winner of no less than eight Tony Awards. With a background in both classical dance and vaudeville, he got his first big break choreographing *The Pajama Game* in 1954, and the film of the same name in 1957.

PROFILE: **BOB FOSSE**

Born: Robert Louis Fosse, 23 June 1927, Chicago
Died: 23 September 1987, Washongton DC.

Major Shows: Pajama Game (1954), How To Succeed In Business Without Really Trying (1961), Sweet Charity (1966), Chicago (1975)

Major Films: Pajama Game (1967), Sweet Charity (1968), Cabaret (1972), All That Jazz (1979)

Fosse's triumphs spanned decades, with his work on the 1972 film of *Cabaret* earning him an Academy Award. His most enduring work was *Chicago*, which was revived in 1996 with choreography (by Ann Reinking) "in the style of Bob Fosse."

A show simply entitled *Fosse* opened on Broadway in 1999, a retrospective of his dance numbers recalling the vitality of his style. It was choreographed by Ann Reinking and Chet Walker, with Broadway veteran and Fosse collaborator Gwen Verdon as artistic advisor.

LEGENDARY MUSICALS:

CABARET

Adapted from a 1951 stage play entitled *I am a Camera* (in itself from Christopher Isherwood's *Goodbye To Berlin* stories about Sally Bowles), the 1966 musical was a radical evocation of Thirties Berlin, notable for the performance of Joel Grey as the Master of Ceremonies of the Kit Kat Club. It was a pert he would repeat to even greater acclaim in the 1972 film, and yet again in a Broadway revival in 1987.

Lyrics: Fred Ebb
Music: John Kander
Book: Joe Masteroff, based on Christopher Isherwood's Berlin stories and John van Druten's play *I am a Camera*.

First Performance:
New York, 20 November 1966, Broadhurst Theater (1165 performances)
London, 28 February 1968, Palace Theatre, (336 performances)

Hit songs: *'Cabaret', 'Willkommen', 'Tomorrow Belongs To Me', 'So What', 'Sitting Pretty (The Money Song)'*

Film version: 1972 (Liza Minelli, Michael York, Joel Grey. Director Bob Fosse)

The first-run production of *Cabaret* won eight Tony Awards, for Best Musical, Supporting Actor (Joel Grey), Supporting Actress (Peg Murray), Score, Director-Producer (Hal Prince), Choreographer (Ron Field), Scenic Design (Boris Aronson) and Costumes (Patricia Zipprodt).

The Master of Ceremonies in the 1986 West End revival of *Cabaret* was played by the British ballet star Wayne Sleep.

In a radically changed production of *Cabaret* in 1993, actress Jane Horrocks had Sally Bowles singing in a deliberately sub-standard, almost out-of-tune fashion, just as she was described as doing in the Isherwood stories.

LEGENDARY MUSICALS:
A CHORUS LINE

One of the most successful musicals of all time, *A Chorus Line* could be considered highly experimental in its whole concept. It dealt with the ritual of chorus dance auditions where Broadway "gypsies" (so-called because they go from show to show) try for their next job, and for his material Michael Bennett drew on a series of taped interview sessions he'd conducted with actual dancers, before collaborating with lyricist Edward Kleban and classically-based composer Marvin Hamlisch.

Lyrics: Edward Kleban
Music: Marvin Hamlisch

Book: Nicholas Dante and James Kirkwood, from a concept by Michael Bennett

First Performance: *New York, 21 May 1975, Public Theater, transferring to the Shubert (6137 performances)*
London, 22 July 1976, Theatre Royal, (903 performances)

Hit songs: *'One', 'At The Ballet', 'I Can Do That', 'What I Did For Love'*

Film version: 1985 (Michael Douglas, Alyson Reed. Director Richard Attenborough)

"I was always drawn to Broadway musicals, and obviously composers like Gershwin, Rodgers, Berlin and Porter were writing music that I found wildly impressive. "
Marvin Hamlisch

·····THE BRITISH ARE COMING!·····

The big British breakthough as far as Broadway was concerned came on 12 October 1971 when *Jesus Christ Superstar* debuted at the Mark Helliger Theater. Its initial run of 711 perform-ances wasn't the longest in history, and was eclipsed by the 3358 shows in London's West End starting the following August. But although there had been hit UK shows in New York before them, *Superstar* began an unprecedented string of successes for writers Tim Rice and Andrew Lloyd Webber, followed by the seemingly never-ending output of hit shows by Lloyd Webber and other collaborators.

"It doesn't stand up to huge intellectual scrutiny."
Andrew Lloyd Webber

PROFILE: **ANDREW LLOYD WEBBER**

Born: 22 March 1948, London

Major Shows: Jesus Christ Superstar (1972), Evita (1976), Cats (1981), Starlight Express (1984), The Phantom of the Opera (1986)

Major Films: Jesus Christ Superstar (1973), Evita (1996), The Phantom of the Opera (2004)

Memorable Songs: I Don't Know How To Love Him (1972), Don't Cry For Me Argentina, Oh What A Circus (1976), All I Ask Of You (1986), Love Changes Everything (1989)

LLOYD WEBBER'S WINNERS

ORIGINAL DATE / SHOW / CO-WRITERS

1968 **Joseph and the Amazing Technicolor Dreamcoat** Tim Rice

1972 **Jesus Christ Superstar** Tim Rice

1975 **By Jeeves** Alan Ayckbourn

1976 **Evita** Tim Rice

1981 **Cats** (based on T. S. Eliot)

1982 **Song and Dance** Don Black

1984 **Starlight Express** Richard Stilgoe

1986 **Phantom of the Opera** Richard Stilgoe/ Charles Hart

1989 **Aspects of Love** Don Black/Charles Hart

1993 **Sunset Boulevard** Don Black/Christopher Hampton

1997 **Whistle Down the Wind** Jim Steinman

2000 **The Beautiful Game** Ben Elton

2004 **The Woman in White** David Zippel

With *Jesus Christ Superstar* and *Joseph and the Amazing Technicolor Dreamcoat*, Rice and Lloyd Webber became the only songwriting team to write successful shows based on both Old Testament and New Testament Biblical subjects.

The peak of the "British Invasion" by Lloyd Webber undoubtedly came with *The Phantom of the Opera*. With a high-tech production by Hal Prince, and co-produced by the composer and British impressario Cameron Mackintosh, the spectacular show dwarfed the Broadway competition when it opened in 1988. Starring Michael Crawford and Sarah Brightman, just as *Cats* had forced *42nd Street* to evacuate the Winter Garden six years before, *Phantom* pushed *42nd Street* out of the Majestic Theatre and over to the St. James.

> *"I can't be a wife. I'm not that sort of person.*
> *Wives have to compromise all the time."*
> Sarah Brightman, Lloyd Webber leading lady and wife
> for six years

Lloyd Webber's original partner Tim Rice didn't sit on his hands after their parting company. His musical *Chess* (1986), written with ex-Abba members Benny Andersson and Bjorn Ulvaeus, was a huge hit in the West End with 1209 performances. It fared less well on Broadway however, where it closed as a "£5 million flop" after just 68 shows in 1988.

Rice hit New York again in 1994 with additional songs (written with composer Alan Menken) for *Beauty and the Beast*. Still running after nearly 5000 shows, it was the first stage show by Walt Disney Productions, based on the animated film. It was something of a Broadway breakthrough for corporate-driven "family" entertainment, where parents would happily take the kids, though the show was scorned by the critics.

Making as much out of souvenir marketing as the actual ticket sales, the success of *Beauty and the Beast* was repeated – and more so – with *Lion King*. Opening in 1997, the spin-off from the 1994 movie was the biggest Broadway show of the decade, with songs written by Elton John and Tim Rice.

For his part in the music of *The Lion King* movie, Tim Rice won an Oscar, a Golden Globe Award, plus an Ivor Novello Award for the song 'Circle of Life'. Rice had earlier scored a Golden Globe and Oscar (with Alan Menken) for the song 'A Whole New World' from their score of the 1992 Walt Disney movie *Alladin*.

THE BLOOD BROTHERS SAGA

Another British success on Broadway was Willy Russell's *Blood Brothers*, which is still running in London after more than twenty years. The story tells of two Liverpool-born twin brothers, separated at birth, who grown up as close friemds not knowing their family relationship.It started life as a youth theatre production for performance in schools, and ended up in the West End, Broadway and theatres worldwide.

1st performance: Fazakerley Comprehensive School Liverpool, November 1981
Liverpool: Playhouse Theatre, 8 January 1983
London: Lyric Theatre, 11 April 1983 Albery Theatre, 28 July 1988 Phoenix Theatre, 1991 (7296+ and still running)
New York: Music Box Theater, 25 April 1993 (1st run 839 performances)

Awards:
1993 Tony Awards – five nominations for Best Musical, Best Book, Best Actor in a Musical, Best Actress in a Musical, Best Featured Actress in a Musical and Best Direction of a Musical

1993 Olivier Award for Best New Musical
1993 Theatre World Award to lead actress Stephanie Lawrence

Blood Brothers **actresses have included:**
Barbara Dickson: Society of West End Theatres Award, Best Actress in a Musical 1983
Stephanie Lawrence: London then Broadway, Tony nomination as Best Actress in a Musical
Helen Reddy: Broadway and West End
Petula Clark: Broadway and US tour
Kiki Dee: West End and UK tour
Carole King: Broadway

Blood Brothers **actors have included:**
David Cassidy: With half brother Shaun played opposite Petula Clark on Broadway
Russell Crowe: Australian production 1988/89
David Soul: Tours of New Zealand, Australia, France and the UK

☆

······················· TRUE TO LIFE? ·····················

The true-life stories of famous people, more often than not quite unconnected with the world of music, have long been the subject of musicals. Among the well-known examples such as P.T. Barnum in *Barnum* and the Argentinian folk hero Eva Peron in *Evita*, here are some more obscure biographies to hit the musical stage.

Summer Song (1956)
(Eric Maschwitz and Hy Kraft, music Antonin Dvorak).
Based on the life of 19th century Czech composer Antonin Dvorak

Gypsy (1959)
Stephen Sondheim, music Jule Styne)
From the autobiography of burlesque stripper Gypsy Rose Lee.

Funny Girl (1964)
(Bob Merrill and Isobel Lennart, music Jule Styne)
Musical biography of the great Broadway vaudeville star Fanny Brice.

Man Of Magic (1966)
(John Morley and Aubrey Cash, music Wilfred Wylam)
The famed escapologist Harry Houdini

Mrs. Wilson's Diary (1967)
(Richard Ingrams and John Wells, music by Jeremy Taylor)
Based on a satirical column in *Private Eye* magazine supposedly written by Prime Minister Harold Wilson's wife.

Sing A Rude Song (1970)
(Caryl Brahms, Ned Sherrin and Alan Bennett, music by Ron Grainer)
The life of British music hall star Marie Lloyd.

I And Albert (1972)
(Jay Allen and Lee Adams, music Charles Strouse)
The relationship of Queen Victoria and consort Prince Albert

Thomas And The King (1975)
(Edward Anhalt and James Herbert, music John Williams)
The troubled relationship of Thomas a Beckett and King Henry II

Evita (1978)
(Tim Rice and Andrew Lloyd Webber)
Depicting the charismatic wife of Argentinian dictator Juan Peron.

Barnardo (1980)
(Ernest Maxin)
The children's home founder Dr Barnardo, inappropriately celebrated in song and dance.

Barnum (1980)
(Michael Stewart and Mark Bramble, music Cy Coleman,)
A hit musical about the showman P.T. Barnum of Barnum and
Bailey's Circus.

The Biograph Girl (1980)
(Warner Brown and David Heneker)
The early days of cinema through the eyes of silent stars Mary
Pickford and Lilian Gish, director D.W. Griffith and studio boss
Adolph Zukor

The Mitford Girls (1981)
(Caryl Brahms and Ned Sherrin)
An unsuccessful attempt to thread a musical into the celebrated
life of the six Mitford sisters

Always (1997)
(William May and Jason Sprague, plus. Frank Hauser and
Debbie Williams)
The love story of abdicated King Edward VIII and Wallace
Simpson.

PROFILE: **STEPHEN SONDHEIM**

Born: Stephen Joshua Sondheim, 22 March 1930, New
York City

Major Shows: West Side Story (1957), Gypsy (1959), A
Funny Thing Happened on the Way to the Forum (1962),
Company (1970), Follies (1971), A Little Night Music
(1973), Side By Side By Sondheim (1976), Sweeney Todd
(1979), Bounce (1999)

Major Films: West Side Story (1961), Gypsy (1962), A
Funny Thing Happened on the Way to the Forum (1966),
A Little Night Music (1978)

*"One difference between poetry and
lyrics is that lyrics
sort of fade into the background.
They fade on the page and live
on the stage when set to music."*
Stephen Sondheim

Memorable Songs: America, Tonight, Maria, Somewhere,
I Feel Pretty (1957), Let Me Entertain You (1959), Love
Will See us Through (1971), Send In The Clowns (1978)

Side By Side By Sondheim, first produced at the Mermaid
Theatre London on 4 May 1976 was a unique piece of musical
theatre, a celebration of Stephen Sondheim's work in the form
of a revue in two acts. With music and lyrics by Stephen
Sondheim plus music by Leonard Bernstein, Mary Rodgers,
Richard Rodgers and Jule Styne, the show moved to
Wyndham's Theatre in the July. The original cast of Millicent
Martin, Julia McKenzie, David Kernan and narrator Ned
Sherrin took the show to New York's Music Box Theatre, on
18 April 1977.

*'I wish life were more like a musical, so when
I burst into song at the bus stop, people would stop staring at me.
It might also make them more inclined to learn the chorus
and the dance numbers."*
P. B. Hill

*"A lot of people are going to hate me for saying this, but one
of my least favorite kinds of music, or the kind of music that
I feel I've so got out of my system, is musicals music."*
Actor Guy Pearce

*"We all sing about the things we're thinking; musicals are
about expressing those emotions that you can't talk about.
It works a real treat."*
Actor Anthony Stewart Head

*"I only wish the British could make adult movies as
intelligent as this one"*
critic Michael Billington reviewing Alan Parker's musical
Bugsy Malone which featured an all-children cast

*"Although Pal Joey is expertly done, can you
draw sweet water from a foul well?"*
critic Brooks Atkinson

*"The toughest thing about success is that you've
got to keep on being a success. "*
Irving Berlin

*"I realized that I was getting older. I had to prioritize what I really
wanted to do in the world of music. I concluded that I wanted to use
my time to write shows for Broadway"*
Marvin Hamlisch

CHART HITS FROM THE SHOWS

Of the ten entries from the US and UK Top Five record
charts listed below, only one ('People') was sung by a
member of the original stage cast.

Rose Marie Slim Whitman, 1955
UK#1 (from *Rose Marie* 1924)
Stranger In Paradise Tony Bennett, 1955
UK#1 (from *Kismet* 1953)
On The Street Where You Live Vic Damone, 1956
US#4,UK#1(from *My Fair Lady* 1956)
Smoke Gets In Your Eyes Platters, 1959
US#1,UK#1 (from *Roberta* 1933)
Where Or When Dion & The Belmonts, 1960
US#3 (from *Babes In Arms*, 1937)
You'll Never Walk Alone Gerry & The Pacemakers, 1963
UK#1 (from *Carousel* 1945)
Hello Dolly Louis Armstrong, 1964
US#1,UK#4 (from *Hello Dolly* 1964)
People Barbra Streisand, 1964
US#5 (from *Funny Girl* 1964)
Aquarius/Let The Sun Shine In 5th Dimension, 1969
US#1 (from *Hair* 1967)
Don't Cry For Me Argentina Julie Covington, 1976
UK#1 (from *Evita* 1978)

NB: Tim Rice and Andrew Lloyd Webber's *Evita* first
appeared as a concept album, two years before it was
produced on the stage, hence Julie Covington's chart entry
with 'Don't Cry For Me Argentina' in 1976. Madonna had
a UK entry with the same song, from the 1996
film version in which she played the title role.

BEST LITTLE SHOW ON BROADWAY

Originally produced at the Actor's Studio in New York on 20 October 1977, if only by virtue of its subject matter and title, *The Best Little Whorehouse in Texas* proved a landmark in stage musicals. It was based on the true story of a brothel known as The Chicken Ranch that existed for over a century in Texas, only to be closed down after a zealous TV reporter featured an exposé on it. The musical moved to the Entermedia Theater, New York, in April 1978, before relocating yet again to the 46th Street Theater on Broadway in the June, where it enjoyed a run of 1584 performances before closing in March 1982.

Written byLarry F.King with songs by Carol Hall, the show was made into a Hollywood film in 1982, starring Dolly Parton and Burt Reynolds. Dolly added two of her own compositions to the score, one of which – 'I Will Always Love You' – made it to No1 in the Country Music charts and was a huge mainstream hit for Whitney Houston a decade later. Used to facing a media perhaps sensitive to the title, DollyParton usually refers to the movie as "The Best Little Chicken House" or "Bleep-house, in Texas."

THE FRENCH CONNECTION

One of the most successful teams to hit Broadway, like Lloyd Webber and his collaborators, was also an import from Europe. Frenchmen Alain Boublil and Claude-Michel Schönberg were responsible for three major shows of the Nineties, *Les Miserables*, *Miss Saigon* and *Martin Guerre*.

Based on the book by Victor Hugo, "Les Mis" (as *Les Miserables* became known colloqually) became the third-longest running West End show in 1994, and now occupies the number two spot in the most performances chart, with over 8000 shows and still running. On Broadway, where it won three Tonys, it also clocked up the third greatest number of performances to date.

Les Miserables was first produced in London in a partly-subsidised form by the Royal Shakespeare Company, who still receive a royalty from the Cameron Mackintosh production company.

BOUBIL AND SCHÖNBERG'S BIG THREE

Les Miserables
Paris: Palais des Sports, 17 September 1980
(107 performances)
London: Barbican Centre, 30 September 1985
(63 performances),
transferred to Palace Theatre, 4 December 1985
(7558+ and still running)
New York: Broadway Theater, 12 March 1987
(6680 performances)

Miss Saigon
London: Drury Lane Theatre, 20 September 1989
(4264 performances)
New York: Broadway Theater, 11 April 1991
(4097 performances)

Martin Guerre
London: Prince Edward Theatre, 10 July 1996
(768 performances)

THE RENT PHENOMENON

One of the most successful musicals of recent years and far removed from the conventional feel-good theme of most song-and-dance stage productions, *Rent* opened at the Theater Workshop in New York on 23 February 1996.

A modern day rock-tinged version of Puccini's opera *La Bohème* and set on Manhattan's Lower East Side, it's the story of a group of bohemian artists struggling to live and enjoy a creative existence in the face of death and AIDS at the end of the 20th century.

On the encouragement of his mentor Stephen Sondheim, writer Jonathan Larson applied for a grant from the Richard Rogers foundation, receiving $45,000 to fund the originally workshop production.

Quite coincidentally, and unbeknown to the writer or cast, the night the show was to open was the 100th anniversay of the original *La Bohème*. The *New York Times* got wind of this, and interviewed Jon Larson the night of the final dress rehearsal. Feeling ill, he returned home immediately after the interview, and died of an aortic aneurism an hour later.

Among many awards, *Rent* won the 1996 Purlitzer Prixe for Drama, and four Tonys the same year, for Best Musical, Best Score, Best Book (both to writer Jonathan Larson) and Best Featured Actor in a Musical (Wilson Jermaine Heredia). It also won the prestigious New York Drama Critics Circle Award in 1996.

After transferring to the Nederlander Theater in March '96, *Rent* went on the clock up over 4,000 perfromances and is still running there.

REAL LIFE

A recent example of real-life biography as a musical was staged at the UK's Chichester Festival in the summer of 2005. Written by Edward Kemp with music & lyrics by Jason Carr, *Six Pictures of Lee Miller* was inspired by Antony Penrose's book on his mother *The Lives of Lee Miller*, the story of a remarkable women whose modelling, photography and journalism took her from the pages of *Vogue* and the Paris of the 30s to the London blitz and the liberation of the Dachau death camp

THE TONY AWARDS

The Tony Awards are presented by Tony Award Productions, a joint venture of the League of American Theatres and Producers, and the American Theatre Wing. Launched on Easter Sunday, 6 April 1947, at a debut dinner in the Grand Ballroom of the Waldorf Astoria hotel, the awards were founded by the American Theatre Wing, an organisation, in its own words, "devoted to promoting excellence in the American theatre." The Awards were so named after Antoinette Perry, an actress, director, producer and the dynamic wartime leader of the American Theatre Wing, who had died shortly before the inception of the Awards.

Although the Tony Awards were established in 1947, the Best Musical category didn't start until two years later, when *Kiss Me Kate* was the winner of the honour. Since 1971, the award has gone to the producer, with the authors of the musical competing in their own categories (Book of a Musical Score).

BEST MUSICAL AWARD, YEAR-BY-YEAR

1949	Kiss Me Kate
1950	South Pacific
1951	Guys and Dolls
1952	The King and I
1953	Wonderful Town
1954	Kismet
1955	The Pyjama Game
1956	Damn Yankees
1957	My Fair Lady
1958	The Music Man
1959	Redhead
1960	The Sound of Music / Fiorello (Joint Winners)
1961	Bye Bye Birdie
1962	How To Succeed in Business Without Really Trying
1963	A Funny Thing Happened on the Way to the Forum
1964	Hello Dolly
1965	Fiddler on the Roof
1966	Man of La Mancha

1967	Cabaret
1968	Hallelujah Baby
1969	1776
1970	Applause
1971	Company
1972	Two Gentlemen of Verona
1973	A Little Night Music
1974	Raisin
1975	The Wiz
1976	A Chorus Line
1977	Annie
1978	Ain't Misbehavin'
1979	Sweeney Todd
1980	Evita
1981	42nd Street
1982	Nine
1983	Cats
1984	La Cage Aux Folles
1985	Big River
1986	The Mystery of Edwin Drood
1987	Les Miserables
1988	The Phantom of the Opera
1989	Jerome Robbins' Broadway
1990	City of Angels
1991	The Will Rogers Follies
1992	Crazy For You
1993	Kiss of the Spider Woman
1994	Passion
1995	Sunset Boulevard
1996	Rent
1997	Titanic
1998	The Lion King
1999	Fosse
2000	Contact
2001	The Producers
2002	Thoroughly Modern Millie
2003	Hairspray
2004	Avenue Q
2005	Monty Python's Spamalot

TOPS IN THE TONYS

Most Nominated:
The Producers (2001) had 15 nominations, winning 12 categories including Best Musical

Most Nominated Revivals:
Kiss Me, Kate (2000), with 12 nominations (of which it won five), then *Anything Goes* (1988), *Show Boat* (1995), *Cabaret* (1998), and *Into the Woods* (2002), each of which received 10 nominations.

Most Won (Musical):
The Producers (2001) won in 12 categories:
Actor (featured role-musical), Actor (musical), Actress (Featured Role-Musical) Book (Musical) Choreographer Costume Designer, Director (Musical), Lighting Designer, Musical, Orchestrations, Original Musical Score, Scenic Designer

Most Won (Composer):
Stephen Sondheim with seven Tony Awards: Best Music and Best Lyrics for *Company* (1971); and Best Score for *Follies* (1972), *A Little Night Music* (1973), *Sweeney Todd* (1979), *Into the Woods* (1988) and *Passion* (1994).

Most Won (Choreographer):
Bob Fosse with eight Awards for choreography: *The Pajama Game* (1955), *Damn Yankees* (1956), *Redhead* (1959), *Little Me* (1963), *Sweet Charity* (1966), *Pippin* (1973), *Dancin'* (1978), and *Big Deal* (1986), plus one for direction, *Pippin* (1973).

Most Won (Actress in a Musical)
Gwen Verdon won the Award four times, for *Can-Can* (1954), *Damn Yankees* (1956), *New Girl in Town* (1958) and *Redhead* (1959)
Angela Lansbury also won four times, for *Mame* (1966), *Dear World* (1969), *Gypsy* (1975), and *Sweeney Todd* (1979)

Mary Martin also received four Tonys: three for performing with *South Pacific* (1950), *Peter Pan* (1955) and *The Sound of Music* (1960), and a special Tony Award in 1948 for "spreading theatre to the rest of the country while the originals perform in New York."

Most Won (Scenic Designer)
Oliver Smith, who collected eight Awards over a nine year period, six of which were for musicals: *My Fair Lady* (1957), *West Side Story* (1958), *The Sound of Music* (1960), *Camelot* (1961), *Hello, Dolly!* (1964) and *Baker Street* (1965).

Design "Triple Crown" (Best Scenic Design of a Musical, Best Costume Design of a Musical, and Best Lighting Design of a Musical)
The coveted "triple crown" of Tony design awards has been achieved by five shows: *Follies* (1972), *The Phantom of the Opera* (1988), *The Lion King* (1998), *The Producers* (2001), and *The Light in the Piazza* in 2005.

Actress **Dolores Gray** performed the shortest-lived Tony Award-winning role. She won the Award for her performance in *Carnival in Flanders* (1953), a musical that ran for only six performances.

Two winners of the Tony **Best Musical Award** have also gone on to win the Oscar for Best Picture in their movie version: *My Fair Lady* (a Tony in 1957, Oscar in 1964) and *The Sound of Music* (Tony 1960, Oscar 1965). And although the original Broadway production of *Chicago* didn't win any Tony Awards in 1976, in 1997 a new production won the Tony as Best Revival, with an Oscar-winning Best Picture following in 2002.

Michael Blakemore is the only director to win Tony Awards as Best Director of a Play and Best Director of a Musical in the same year. He won for both the play *Copenhagen* and musical *Kiss Me, Kate* in 2000.

Bob Fosse was the only director to win a Tony, an Oscar, and an Emmy in the same year (1973). He won two Tonys (direction and choreography) for *Pippin*, an Oscar for *Cabaret* plus an Emmy for "Liza with a Z."

Lauri Peters shared a single 1960 nomination as Best Featured Actress in a Musical with Kathy Dunn, Evanna Lien, Mary Susan Locke, and Marilyn Rogers – plus two boys, William Snowden, and Joseph Stewart. They played various younger Von Trapp children in the original production of *The Sound of Music*.

Despite its enormous success in every other respect, the musical that fared most poorly in a Tony ceremony was *Chicago* in 1976, which received eleven nominations but failed to collect even one award. It was up against *A Chorus Line*, which came out on top in nine of the musical categories.

Chicago's poor showing of 0 out of 11 was repeated again the following year by *Steel Pier*, with a score by the same team of John Kander and Fred Ebb. But this time it was Chicago that dominated the winners, with six awards coming its way on Tony night.

THE OLIVIER AWARDS

The British equivalent to the Tony awards are the
Laurence Olivier Theatre Awards, which were started
in 1976. Listed below, the winners in the **Best New
Musical** category.

1976	A Chorus Line
1977	The Comedy of Errors
1978	Evita
1979	Songbook
1980	Sweeney Todd
1981	Cats
1982	Poppy
1983	Blood Brothers
1984	42nd Street
1985	Me and My Girl
1986	The Phantom of the Opera
1987	Follies
1988	Candide
1989/90	Return to the Forbidden Planet
1991	Sunday in the Park with George
1992	Carmen Jones (revival)
1993	Crazy For You
1994	City of Angels
1995	Once On This Island
1996	Jolson The Musical
1997	Martin Guerre
1998	Beauty and The Beast
1999	Kat and The Kings
2000	Honk! The Ugly Duckling
2001	Merrily We Roll Along
2003	Our House
2004	Jerry Springer – The Opera
2005	The Producers

"LET'S PUT ON A MUSICAL!"

From the works of Gilbert and Sullivan onwards, musicals have been a great source of material for that phenomenon known as amateur dramatics. Schools, women's groups, charity organisations and just the ubiquitous local Dramatic Society all have a go at everything from G&S to *The Sound of Music*, often bravely regardless of the level of musical ability among the eager cast.

CHOOSING A SHOW

A website offering advice to amateur groups as to which musical to choose includes the following (often amusing) recommendations:

Musicals with Parts for Middle-Aged Performers
La Cage aux Folles / Company / Do I Hear a Waltz? / Is There Life After High School? / On a Clear Day, You Can See Forever / The Pajama Game

Musicals with Jewish Appeal
Fiddler on the Roof / The Grand Tour / I Can Get It for You Wholesale / Milk and Honey / Rags

Musicals for Sophisticated Communities
Assassins / The Best Little Whorehouse in Texas / Cabaret / The Cradle Will Rock / Sunday in the Park with George / Sweeney Todd, the Demon Barber of Fleet Street

Musicals for Ethnic and Minority Casts
Dreamgirls / Flower Drum Song / Golden Boy / Grind / Miss Saigon / Once on this Island / Purlie / Raisin / The Wiz

Cult Shows That Haven't Yet Found Their Audience
Anyone Can Whistle / Baby / Birds of Paradise / The Happy Time / Mack & Mabel / She Loves Me / Working

Musicals That Can Be Done on a Small Budget

Don't Bother Me, I Can't Cope / The Fantasticks / I Do, I Do /
Jacques Brel Is Alive and Well and Living in Paris / Romance,
Romance / Stop the World – I Want to Get Off

USEFUL BOOKS FOR AMATEUR GROUPS

(Title / Author / Publisher)

Let's Put on a Musical! / Peter Filichia / Back Stage (US)

Play Director's Survival Kit / James W. Rodgers and Wanda C.
Rodgers / Jossey-Bass (US)

Technical Theater for Nontechnical People / Drew
Campbell / Allworth (US)

Play Directing in the School / David Grote / Meriwether
(US)

How to Direct a Musical / David Young / Routledge
(US/UK)

Create Your Own Stage Effects / Gill Davies / Back Stage
(US) A&C Black (UK)

Making Stage Props: A Practical Guide / Andy Wilson /
Crowood Press (UK)

**Instant Period Costume: How to Make Classic Costumes
from Cast-Off Clothing** / Barb Rogers / Meriwether (US)

BIBLIOGRAPHY AND SOURCES

Driver, Ian: *A Century of Dance* [Hamlyn, UK 2000]

Evans, Mike: *NYC Rock* [Sanctuary, UK 2003]

George-Warren, Holly [contributor]: *New York City: Traditions*
[Hamlyn, UK 1998]

Gow, Gordon: *Hollywood in the Fifties* [AS Barnes, US 1971]

Higham, Charles & Greenberg, Joel:
Hollywood in the Forties [AS Barnes, US 1968]

Jackson, Arthur: *The Book of Musicals*
[Mitchell Beazley, UK 1977]

Kennedy, Michael Patrick & Muir, John: *Musicals*
[Harper Collins, UK 1997]

Larkin, Colin: *Encyclopaedia of Stage and Film Musicals*
[Virgin, UK 2000]

Palmer, Tony: *All You Need Is Love*
[Weidenfeld & Nicholson, UK 1976]

Vena, Gary [contributor]: *New York City: Traditions*
[Hamlyn, UK 1998]

Walker, John [ed]: *Halliwell's Film & Video Guide*
[Harper Collins, UK 2001]

Walker, John [ed]: *Halliwell's Who's Who in the Movies*
[Harper Collins, UK 2001]

Wallock, Leonard [ed]: *New York: Culture Capital of the World*
[Rizzoli, US lgg81

Whitcomb, Ian: *After The Ball* [Penguin, UK 1973]

Websites

musicalslOl.com

world-theatres.com

*"The musicals had a good, happy feeling,
saying that the world is a better place"*
Shirley Jones